HOW TO TAKE
GREAT
PHOTOGRAPHS

HOW TO TAKE
GREAT
PHOTOGRAPHS
A Practical Photography Course

JOHN FREEMAN

ACROPOLIS BOOKS

First published in 1995 by Lorenz Books

Photographs © John Freeman
© Anness Publishing Limited 1995

Lorenz Books is an imprint of
Anness Publishing Limited
1 Boundary Row
London SE1 8HP

This edition exclusively
distributed in Canada by
Book Express, an imprint of
Raincoast Books Distribution Limited

Distributed in Australia by Reed Editions

Editorial Director Joanna Lorenz
Project Editor Penelope Cream
Designer Michael Morey
Illustrator John Hutchinson

Typeset by MC Typeset Limited
Printed and bound in Singapore

ISBN 1 85967 044 X

CONTENTS

Equipment & Techniques

The question that professional photographers are probably asked most frequently is, 'What is the best camera I can buy?' Unfortunately there is no simple answer. Even though many people consider the Rolls-Royce to be the best motor car in the world, it is not suited to all uses: it would be at a distinct disadvantage in a Formula One race. In the same way, there are some cameras that some photographers consider the 'Rolls-Royce' of their kind yet it does not always follow that these are the best choice for all shooting situations. Undoubtedly the camera that has proved most popular is the 35 mm SLR.

The important aspects to consider when choosing a camera are application, variety of accessories and cost. The range of cameras available is wide, yet each type is very distinct in

its uses. Photographers should examine the different models and decide which might be the most suitable for their requirements. Ultimately, however, whichever camera is used, the elements that go to make up the final image will be those that the photographer brings to the camera, rather than the number of dials or knobs it has. Even a disposable camera can produce a good picture in the hands of an attentive and enthusiastic photographer who takes care with composition, gives thought to foreground and background, and notes the prevailing lighting conditions. Great shots can be achieved with even the most modest budget and a little technical knowledge.

The more money the photographer is prepared to spend, the more sophisticated the camera can be; usually

the different models will include autoexposure and built-in flash (although this may not always be very powerful), motor drive, zoom lens, autofocus, and automatic rewinding of the film back into the cassette when the reel is complete. Models at the cheaper end of the range have a fixed lens and focus limit so that bright daylight conditions are required. The more expensive models obviously expand the creative possibilities of the 35 mm camera, although even the basic models are reliable and will produce effective shots.

THE 35 MM CAMERA
The compact 35 mm camera (so-called because it uses 35 mm film) is an ideal

• The range of 35 mm cameras is enormous, from a disposable model, BOTTOM LEFT, through to the most sophisticated autometering and autofocusing types, FAR RIGHT.

model for those beginning photography or those who want a simple all-in-one with the minimum of accessories and adjustments. There is a vast range of different models within the 35 mm category. The simplest, and cheapest, will be a 'point-and-shoot' version without a built-in exposure meter or flash where the film is loaded and advanced manually.

THE SINGLE REFLEX (SLR) CAMERA

This camera is portable and extremely adaptable. Since its introduction approximately 50 years ago, the SLR (single lens reflex) has proved to be one of the most popular cameras available. The original design has now evolved

into a multiplicity of models, the majority of which have a formidable array of lenses and accessories.

When you look through the viewfinder of an SLR camera what you see is what the lens 'sees'. This is because there is a mirror behind the lens that reflects the image up to a device called a pentaprism. This turns the image the right way up and the correct way round, and is situated on the top of the camera in front of the viewfinder. In normal conditions, when the shutter release button is pressed several functions operate in a fraction of a second. First the mirror flips up 45

degrees so that light can pass through the lens onto the film. The aperture you have chosen stops down. The focal plane shutter opens for the amount of time you have chosen on the shutter speed dial and then closes, then the aperture opens up to its full extent and the mirror comes back down so that you can view the scene again.

Using readily available 35 mm film, the basic SLR model can be adapted by the addition of all sorts of equipment, including telephoto or zoom lenses, motor drive and flash units. This means that it is the ideal 'system' camera; it can be adapted as quickly or as slowly as budget allows. An extra advantage to

EQUIPMENT & TECHNIQUES

the SLR is that the top-of-the-range models and accessories popular with professional photographers can be hired at specialist camera shops. In this way, a vast amount of equipment is available for minimum financial outlay.

THE RANGEFINDER CAMERA

This is another model of camera which has proved very popular with professional photographers. The most famous brand of rangefinder is the Leica; the French photojournalist Henri Cartier-Bresson shot nearly all his most memorable pictures using one.

In contrast to the SLR camera, the rangefinder allows the subject to be seen through a separate viewfinder rather than through the lens. In the centre of the viewfinder are two images. When the lens is focused on the subject these two images become aligned with one another and the picture will then be sharp. This method of working is preferred by some photographers who find that the camera is quieter to operate and is less prone to being affected by vibration as there is no mirror to flip up. Although the rangefinder does not have quite as wide

a range of accessories as the SLR, it is a sturdy and reliable camera with extremely high-quality lenses. The rangefinder is available in 35 mm or medium format models.

THE SLR MEDIUM FORMAT CAMERA

These cameras come between the 35 mm and the large format cameras in size and application. They take pictures in a variety of formats including 6 × 4.5 cm, 6 × 6 cm and 6 × 7 cm. These cameras have extensive ranges of lenses and accessories and are much favoured by professional photographers. They are much bulkier than 35 mm cameras and are usually used on a tripod, although they can be hand-held. They are the only cameras that use 120 or 220 ISO film, available in roll or cassette form.

THE 5 × 4 CAMERA

This is a large format, tripod-mounted camera which takes photographs where the transparencies or negatives are 5 × 4 in (12.5 × 10 cm). The film is loaded into dark slides, each one holding just two sheets. There is no viewfinder in the conventional sense: the image is seen upside-down and back-to-front on a ground glass screen. In order to see the image and keep out any stray light the photographer covers the camera and his head with a dark cloth. Despite the rather old-fashioned appearance of the camera, many models are in fact brand-new, extremely sophisticated and can be very expensive.

The range of applications of the 5 × 4 camera is very varied both in the studio and on location. It produces pictures with excellent clarity and sharpness of detail. However, it would

● Medium format and large format cameras, such as the 5 × 4 in, FAR RIGHT, are generally favoured by professionals.

not be the best choice for spontaneous or action shots where a more portable camera with speedy shooting capability might be more suitable.

THE INSTANT AND POLAROID CAMERA

Instant picture cameras such as the Polaroid offer another dimension to picture-taking. After the picture is taken, the film is impregnated with the chemicals required for processing the image and the picture begins to appear only seconds after the shutter is pressed; development is complete within minutes. As well as providing an immediate image of the subject, these cameras also offer as many possibilities for creative photography as their conventional counterparts. Many professional photographers attach special Polaroid backs to their standard cameras; once they have composed the image and calculated the exposure they will take a Polaroid picture to ensure everything is perfect before shooting on conventional film. Polaroid backs are available for all cameras from 35 mm size to 10 × 8 models.

THE VIDEO STILL CAMERA

The video still camera is a relatively new type of camera; it uses a computer disk instead of conventional film and the pictures can be viewed on a television screen or video monitor, or sent away to be made into prints. Although still in its early stages, this form of photography could change the nature of picture-taking in the future.

EQUIPMENT: LENSES

Just as there is no one camera that is ideal for every shooting situation, the same is true of lenses. Some lenses in certain situations have distinct advantages over others. An extra element of challenge can be added to photography by experimentation with different lenses, perhaps applying a particular lens to a situation in which it is not normally used.

LENSES FOR 35 MM SLR CAMERAS

Most 35 mm SLR cameras are purchased with what is known as a 'standard' lens. This has a focal length of about 50 mm and will give an angle of view roughly equivalent to what we see with our own eyes. Its maximum aperture in the region of f1.8, but faster lenses such as f1.4 and f1.2 are

available. At a later date one of these faster lenses could prove useful.

LENS MOUNTS

All SLR cameras have interchangeable lenses, attached to the camera by means of a mount. There are several different sorts of mount, the most popular being the bayonet mount. This is operated by depressing or sliding a small button positioned on the camera body near the

lens. The lens can then be turned 45 degrees in a clockwise direction and pulled gently forward from the camera body, and another lens inserted using the reverse procedure.

CHOICE OF LENSES

Interchangeability of lenses opens up a

● A selection of zoom
and telephoto lenses.

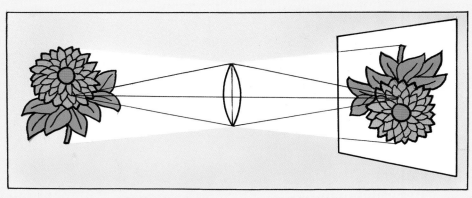

● ABOVE The subject is reproduced through a lens upside-down on the film.

vast array of options and is probably the biggest single factor in improving photographic creativity. Having chosen a camera and standard lens, it is advisable to consider purchasing two other lenses at the same time or very shortly after. These would probably be a wide angle lens in the focal range of 28–35 mm, and a telephoto lens in the 85–135 mm range.

WIDE ANGLE LENSES

A wide angle lens gives a wider angle of view, so more of the area in front of the camera will appear in the shot. Like any piece of equipment there are disadvantages as well as benefits; the

● Wide angle and medium telephoto lenses.

most common in the case of the wide angle lens occurs in landscape photography where the foreground may lack interest so the eye is not naturally led to the central point of the picture.

On the other hand, a wide angle lens allows subjects to be photographed much closer to the lens than usual, while at the same time keeping the background in focus. In some cases this effect can greatly enhance a composition.

TELEPHOTO LENSES

A medium telephoto lens has many advantages. As well as bringing distant objects closer, it is a superb lens for portraits. It has definite advantages over a wide angle lens in this situation as, when used straight onto someone's face, a wide angle lens will add an unflattering, albeit at times amusing, bulbous quality. A telephoto lens in the region of 100 mm enables the photographer to stand some distance away, making the subject more relaxed and allowing an unblocked light source. The lens will very slightly compress the image, making for a far more pleasing portrait. The depth of field will be less, so the background can be put out of focus and a part of the subject's face, such as the eyes, can be highlighted.

ZOOM LENSES

Many photographers find these lenses very convenient; they give the benefit of being adjustable to an infinite variety of focal lengths which can make composition of pictures much easier. Although in a technical sense a zoom lens will not produce the same quality as a prime lens of a given focal length, under most conditions the difference will be apparent only to an eagle eye.

Depending on the type of photography that is of interest, wide angle and telephoto lenses that are of a very extreme range have limited applications and can easily be under-used; their purchase should therefore be considered very seriously.

FISHEYE LENSES

A fisheye lens can be used to dramatic effect, but as an everyday piece of equipment it has limited applications and its novelty value can quickly wear off.

● Ultra-telephoto lenses.

A MACRO LENS

The macro lens allows the photographer to get very close to the subject without the need for special close-up attachments. Depending on the lens used, small objects can be magnified to produce a final print which shows them life-size. Many of the lenses mentioned here in the 28–300 mm range have this facility built in and it is often worth considering paying a bit extra at the outset if this is of interest.

SHIFT OR PERSPECTIVE CONTROL LENS

The shift or perspective control lens allows photography of a subject that is very tall, without the problem of converging verticals; this occurs when the sides of the subject taper toward the top of the picture. The conventional rule for preventing this from happening is to ensure that the film plane is parallel to the vertical plane of the subject and then all vertical lines will remain straight in the final shot. However, with a fixed lens the top of a very tall subject is usually cut off, but with a shift lens the axis can be altered, allowing the camera to remain straight while the lens is moved upwards: the top of the building will then come into view.

● Fisheye, ultra-wide angle and macro lenses.

● BELOW By using a shift, or perspective control, lens, as opposed to moving the camera, subjects such as tall buildings can be perfectly framed.

ACCESSORIES

There are many accessories that can be added to a basic camera unit when building up a comprehensive 'system'. It is important to bear in mind that no accessory on its own is going to provide a magic formula for improving photographic skills. Accessories lend technical help, yet it is the photographer's eye for seeing a good picture that is the essence of photography.

A UV FILTER

Having decided on and purchased the camera, the next thing to buy is an UV filter. This can be kept on the lens at all times, whether you are using colour or black and white film. As well as reducing the amount of ultraviolet light passing through the lens (cutting down haze and minimizing the risk of a blue cast appearing on the film), it will also protect the lens itself. It is much cheaper to replace even a good quality glass filter if it gets scratched than a scratched lens. Consider buying a UV filter for each lens.

As well as the UV filter, there is a whole selection of special filters and holders available. These range from colour correction and colour-balancing filters to special effect filters and masks.

THE LENS HOOD

This should be bought at the same time as the camera. Look at any picture of professional photographers at work and they will all be using lens hoods. The hood prevents most stray light from entering the lens. Stray light causes flare and can ruin the picture. It may be caused by sunlight falling directly into the lens or being reflected off a building or shiny surface. If you are in any doubt as to the necessity of a lens hood, next time you are walking or driving into the sun, notice how you need to shield your eyes from the light with a hand or

the sun visor in the car. A lens hood works in exactly the same way for the camera lens.

A TRIPOD

A tripod keeps the camera steady during shooting at long exposures. To be effective the tripod must be rigid. Some tripods are very flimsy when fully extended so it is often well worth paying a little extra money for a truly sturdy model. Tripods are

available in many sizes from the smallest, which are about 15 cm (6 in) high, to much larger, heavy-duty models which can extend to well over 3 m (10 ft).

Some tripods come complete with all attachments; others need a head, the part that fixes the camera to the tripod. Heads can vary and it is important to look at several before making a final choice. The most common type is the 'pan and tilt' head which allows the

● A combination of accessories aids the able photographer to enhance shots, and to be more versatile in a variety of situations.

adjusted to different heights. Obviously, a monopod will not stand unaided but it can be used to help brace the camera. Professional photographers at a football match, for example, nearly always use a monopod.

A Cable Release

A cable release can be attached to any camera which allows it to be screwed into the shutter release button; when the plunger on the end of the cable is depressed it fires the shutter without the need for any direct manual contact. It is often used in conjunction with a tripod when shooting at slow speeds to reduce the vibration that often occurs when the shutter is released manually.

Some cable releases are now available for SLR cameras. When the cable is depressed half-way the mirror-up mechanism is activated. Any vibration that occurs when the mirror goes up is then eliminated by this intermediate stage in the shutter release process. When the cable plunger is depressed fully the shutter is fired and the camera remains steady.

A Carrying Case

A case to carry all the accessories is convenient and also provides protection for equipment. The most effective cases have hard outer shells, and compartments moulded from foam rubber to hold the individual accessories. Soft cases are also available but these may not be suitable for very delicate items. Many cases are obviously meant for carrying cameras; this attracts thieves, so do lock them out of sight if left in a car. Insuring expensive photographic equipment is becoming increasingly costly; if you think that you may have to leave equipment in a locked vehicle, make sure that the insurance policy covers theft from cars.

camera to be moved smoothly through 360 degrees – the 'pan' movement. At the same time it can be adjusted vertically; this is usually in the range of 90 degrees forwards and 45 degrees backwards – this is the 'tilt' movement. (If an angle of 45 degrees is not sufficient, turn the camera round and use the head back-to-front.)

Another useful head is the 'ball and socket' version. Normally this has two knobs that allow the camera to be

moved when fixed to the tripod in much the same direction as the pan and tilt head, yet is far less cumbersome.

A Monopod

Since many tripods are often bulky, some places such as churches, buildings of historical interest and museums do not allow their use without a permit. One solution to this may be to use a monopod. As its name suggests, it consists of a single leg which can be

Flash guns

Ring flash

FLASH ATTACHMENTS

Most SLR cameras do not have built-in flash so it is certainly worth purchasing a flash unit to attach to the 'hot shoe' or accessory shoe on the camera. Some are quite compact but are nevertheless sophisticated and powerful.

The more powerful flash units are mounted on a bracket that is screwed into the base plate of the camera, and linked to the flash synchronization socket on the camera by means of a cable. When the shutter is activated a signal is sent to fire the flash.

EXPOSURE METERS

Although most cameras now have some sort of built-in mechanism for evaluating exposure, a separate hand-held exposure meter is very useful. Basic photoelectric meters need no batteries and register the amount of light available. Although reliable, they are not as powerful nor as sensitive as the battery-powered meters; many of these can be used as flash meters as well as for reading ambient light.

Bellows

Flash and ambient
light meter

Set of extension rings

Battery-powered
exposure meter

Photoelectric meter

In ambient light mode, they can be used to take incident light readings as well as reflected light readings. An incident light reading is taken when the meter is placed on or near the subject and pointed towards the light source to take a reading. A reflected light reading is taken when the meter is directed at the subject from the camera position.

It will take a little practice to be able to evaluate the various benefits of the different types of reading.

EXTENSION RINGS OR BELLOWS

These are used in conjunction with SLR cameras and allow close-up photography of detail in stunning clarity. Close-up lenses can be used for the same purpose but extension rings give a far better result.

The rings or bellows are attached to the body of the camera on the lens mounting; the lens is then attached to the front of these. The rings offer a single magnification whereas with the bellows the magnification is variable.

CARE OF EQUIPMENT

Cameras and lenses are delicate and expensive instruments that need to be treated with care. Water, dust, dirt and grit are the worst enemies, although leaving a camera in bright sunlight or in the glove compartment of a car will not do it any good either, and so any strong heat should be avoided. If the camera is taken to a sandy beach, keep it wrapped in a plastic bag when not in use. Even on the calmest days sand seems to get into every crack; extra care needs to be taken as sand can easily ruin expensive equipment.

When a camera is not in use it should be kept in its case or together with the other pieces of equipment in a proper camera case. If it is not going to be used for some time the batteries should be removed; if left in the camera they may corrode the contacts and cause irreparable damage.

LENSES AND FILTERS

Always keep a skylight UV filter on the lenses. This will keep out UV light and will help protect the lenses themselves. This filter can be kept on the lenses permanently, with either colour or black and white film. A scratched filter is cheaper to replace than a damaged lens. If the filter or lens becomes dirty first blow away the dust and any other particles of dirt. The most efficient way of doing this is to use a pressurized can of air. Many of these products are ozone-friendly and do not contain CFC propellants. Alternatively, use a soft brush with a blower attached to it. If neither of these pieces of equipment is available, simply blow gently onto the surface. The next stage is to remove any grease by gently wiping the lens or filter with a soft lens tissue or lens cloth.

If something jams in or on the camera and the fault is not apparent never force the piece, as more serious damage could be caused. If the lens or camera develops a serious fault send it

Soft cleaning cloth

Lens cap

Blower brush

UV filter

to a reputable camera repair shop. If it is still under guarantee, return it to the dealer or direct to the manufacturer.

Pressurized air blower

Lens cleaning tissue

Lens cleaning fluid

Cotton buds for cleaning

Negatives and transparencies form an archive of images, preserving memories and moments forever. A visual diary of children can be built up from birth. These children may well have children of their own, and even grandchildren. What better way of seeing a family's development, a history of its background, even the country it has come from, than in a series of photographs? If all the negatives have been kept in good condition, then future generations can assemble a fascinating visual family tree.

It is only too easy to mislay colour negatives and transparencies. This can be a great pity; if prints are destroyed, or friends or relatives would like copies of pictures, others can always be produced from the negatives. While it is possible to reproduce an image from an existing print the quality will not be as good.

STORAGE OF NEGATIVES

Negatives are returned with prints in a wallet. If they are dated and catalogued properly these provide a perfectly adequate storage system. The wallets can be filed in a drawer with a simple log of what they are. Alternatively, special negative storage filing systems are available; these consist of double-thickness plastic or paper sheets with pockets or channels for holding the transparencies. The sheets are then stored in binders or hung from metal rods in filing cabinet drawers.

STORAGE OF TRANSPARENCIES

If they are mounted as slides, transparencies can be stored in slide boxes, grooved to take a mounted slide, with an index for cataloguing the pictures. If the slides are for projection, they can be kept in a slide projector magazine or tray. These have dust covers and can be indexed as before.

Sharp-bladed scissors

35 mm transparency file

Mounted transparencies

Negative storage sheets

6 × 6 cm transparency file

Rigid plastic 35 mm viewing sheets

Negative storage file

There are two main types of colour film used.

● Colour reversal film produces transparencies that can be mounted as slides and projected or viewed with a slide viewer or on a light box. Transparencies can also be made into prints, either directly, or from what is called an internegative, which involves photographing the transparency onto the other kind of film, colour negative film.

● Colour negative film is the type used to make prints.

Most professional photographers use colour reversal film, whereas most amateurs prefer colour negative.

Both types of film come in a full range of sizes, from the small 110 up through 35 mm to 10 × 8 in (30 × 20 cm) sheet film. They also come in various speeds. These are given as an ISO (International Standards Organization) number from about 25 for the slowest up to 1600 and beyond for the fastest. The slower the film, the finer the grain and sharpness, and the greater the colour saturation and contrast. 1600 ISO film can be uprated to 3200 ISO and more for work in low light but the result will be very grainy – an effect which may be sought deliberately.

UPRATING FILM AND DX CODING

Uprating, also called speed readjustment, means using film as if it had a higher ISO rating than it actually does, and so shortening exposure time. Uprated film needs a longer development time, and if you uprate any film you must let the laboratory know that you have done this so that they can 'push', or extend, development. Some laboratories charge extra for handling uprated film. Generally only colour reversal film is uprated since the processing for all colour negative films is the same. However, a few colour negative films are now made in such a way that they can be uprated.

35 mm film is now DX coded: this means that the film cassette has a bar code on it. Nearly all new cameras have tiny sensors that read the code and automatically change the camera's ISO setting to the appropriate speed. If you

want to uprate the film you should buy bar code override stickers to put on the cassette. Alternatively, if your camera has an exposure compensating dial, you can adjust this to uprate the film. In either case you must inform the laboratory of what you have done.

LIGHTING

There are two types of colour reversal film: one for daylight and electronic flash, the other for tungsten light (ordinary lamps). If daylight film is used in tungsten light the shots will come out very warm, with an orange and red glow to them. If tungsten-balanced film is used in daylight the pictures will have a blue cast. Although both these films are made for the specified lighting conditions there is no reason why they should not be used in different lighting to create a special effect. Either of them can also be used with a light-balancing filter. Using an 85B filter, which looks orange, on a camera allows tungsten film to be used in daylight or with electronic flash to get a normal colour balance. An 80B filter, which is bluish, allows daylight film to be used in tungsten film with normal results.

Until recently there was only one kind of colour negative film which was used in both daylight and tungsten light. Any colour cast was corrected at the printing stage. However, there are now several colour negative films available that are made specifically for use in tungsten light.

ACCURATE EXPOSURE

Exposure needs to be far more accurate for colour reversal film than for colour negative because the transparency is the final result. With colour negative film any inaccuracies in the negative can be corrected at the print stage. Where accuracy is required it is a great help to make a test with an instant film such as Polaroid so that any adjustments can be made on the spot.

INFRARED FILM

You might also like to experiment with infrared film. This gives unusual though unpredictable results, quite different from the colours we normally see. For example, foliage becomes magenta and pale skin tones green.

EQUIPMENT & TECHNIQUES

Over the last two decades shooting in colour has become the norm in photography, and amateurs have almost abandoned black and white. This is a great pity, for many colour photographs would look better in monochrome. Some of today's best known photographers, such as Steven Miesels, Herb Ritts and the late Robert Mapplethorpe, are famous for their work in black and white, and exhibitions and books of their work consist almost entirely of black and white prints.

Undoubtedly most people relate immediately to a colour photograph, which is hardly surprising as we see the world in colour. Therefore any colour image is relatively acceptable, while an image in black and white has to be spot on for it to get the attention it deserves. Another reason for the neglect of black and white is that the film is now almost as expensive to buy and more expensive to process than colour. It also takes longer to process: you cannot get your prints back in an hour!

Unlike colour film, which has negative and reversal types, black and white film is almost always negative. There is no need to worry about colour balance, as black and white film can be used under any lighting conditions. It comes in speeds from very slow, such as 25 ISO, to ultra-fast at 3200 ISO – and even this can be 'push processed' to increase the speed still further. Slow film gives very fine grain and good shadow detail, and pictures can be enlarged with little loss of quality. In contrast the faster films are generally very grainy and the shadow detail inferior.

BLACK AND WHITE FILM

When black and white film is processed it is usual to make a contact sheet. This means that, for instance, a 36 exposure roll of film is cut into six strips of six negatives. These are placed on a 10 × 8 in (30 × 20 cm) sheet of printing paper to make a positive print. On this contact sheet you select and mark the negatives you want to have made into enlarged prints. In making this selection you can ask for unwanted parts of the negative to be cropped out — draw the area you want on the contact sheet as a guide. You can also ask the printer to angle the masking frame, which holds the printing paper in place on the enlarger, to tilt the picture. This can often improve the overall composition. Some laboratories can produce enlarged 'contacts' which give a better idea of how enlargements will look. The whole film is printed on a 16 × 12 in (40 × 30 cm), 20 × 16 in (50 × 30 cm) or 24 × 20 in (60 × 50 cm) sheet.

Prints can be ordered in different finishes, from matt to glossy. Paper types include resin-coated, which has a plastic surface that gives faster development, needs less washing and dries faster than the traditional type. The older fibre-based paper, which gives a more subtle effect, is favoured by photographers for exhibitions and portfolios. On both these papers you can have toned prints. Sepia is the best known tone, but there are others. Some are more suitable for fibre-based paper, others for resin-coated. You can also hand colour your prints. This old technique is now enjoying a revival. It calls for special colouring media.

SPECIAL BLACK AND WHITE FILM

Black and white slides for projection are made on special 'positive' black and white film. There is also black and white instant film, made by Polaroid. Infrared black and white film gives unusual results: pictures taken in daylight look like night scenes. This film should be tested before you use it in earnest, to avoid unexpected results.

FILTERS FOR BLACK AND WHITE

Although you do not need to use light balancing filters for black and white film, some coloured filters can add interest to your images. For example, a yellow filter will darken a blue sky and make the clouds stand out sharply. A red filter will exaggerate the effect: even a blue sky with white clouds will look positively stormy.

THE HUMAN EYE AND THE CAMERA

We see the world in colour, so it is hardly surprising that most people tend to load their cameras with colour film. Even before the invention of colour film black and white prints were toned or sometimes hand coloured to add realism.

Technical improvements in colour film have made it possible for everyone to get a reasonably exposed photograph. But exposure is not the only element of a successful colour image. In the same way as a painter controls the colours on his palette, the way we combine colours in photographs, and juxtapose different and complementary hues, plays a vital role in achieving a successful image.

THE HUMAN EYE AND FILM

The colours we see are reflected off the objects we look at. The light that falls on these objects constantly changes, and with it their colours. Daylight is warmer – that is, redder – at the beginning and end of the day than at midday. Weather also changes the quality of daylight. On an overcast day we see colour as cooler – bluer – than in bright sunshine. Hazy sunlight gives muted colours. However, the most

important element in colour vision is not the eye but the brain. If we know that a jacket is a particular shade of red we will see that shade of red at any time of day, in any weather, and even indoors under artificial light – ordinary tungsten bulbs throw out a light strongly biased towards the orange and red end of the spectrum, and give colours markedly different from those produced by sunlight.

Film reacts differently. When we move indoors from daylight our vision adjusts to the change in light quality. But if we load a camera with a film made for use in daylight, and use it to photograph the red jacket first out of doors then indoors under tungsten light, the first shot will look about right but the second shot will have a strong orange cast to it. If we use film balanced for tungsten light, the indoor shot will look fine but the outdoor one will be skewed towards the other end of the spectrum, with a blue-violet cast.

It is important to understand how our eyes record colour, and how colour film does it, and to experiment with these effects, in order to create successful colour photographs.

● The juxtaposition of varied coloured images produces a startlingly vibrant collage of contrasting and complementary shades and tones.

SEEING IN BLACK AND WHITE

EQUIPMENT & TECHNIQUES

Taking photographs in black and white is a most rewarding exercise. It is sad that most people today would not dream of putting anything other than colour film in their cameras. Undoubtedly this is because they want their photographs to record the way they remember a particular scene. Yet the absence of colour in a black and white photograph can make a far more striking interpretation of that scene. And since black and white imagery is an interpretation rather than a mere record, the onus is on the photographer to create a picture through the use of texture and tone; these are important considerations in colour photography, but in black and white they are paramount.

If you have two cameras, try loading one with black and white and the other with colour. When you compare your prints you might be surprised at the power of the black and white images.

TONAL RANGE

The tonal range from black through various shades of grey to white is known as the grey scale. Professional photographic stores sell charts of these scales called step wedges, which can be used to analyse a photograph. A black and white print where most of the tones are from the extremes of the scale —without any mid-tones — is referred to as a high-contrast print. If these tones are mostly towards the white end it is called a high-key picture. A picture where most of the tones are near the black end is a low-key print. One that uses the full range of tones is called a full-tone print.

One of the great exponents of black and white photography was the American Ansel Adams. His landscapes combine stunning composition with a powerful grasp of tonal range. They are worth studying.

● ABOVE This picture emphasizes the soft, velvety appearance of the girl's skin. She is lit using a single studio flash unit fitted with a large diffuser or soft box. As its name suggests, this gives a very soft and even light. The picture was shot on the same film, 100 ISO, as was used for the image of the older man.

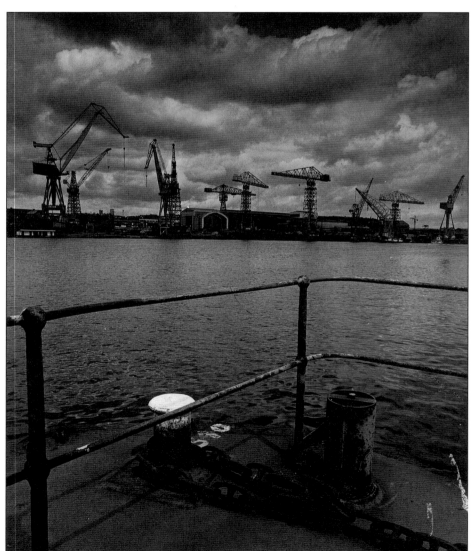

● LEFT By shooting this ship-building dock threatened with closure in black and white, the mood is emphasized much more than it would be in colour. The print was deliberately made darker to reinforce this image of despair.

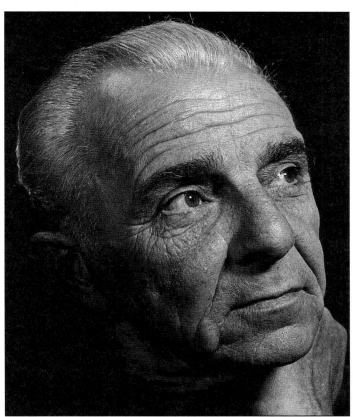

● LEFT This studio picture shows a good tonal range. The black at the extreme end of the scale is rich and even, and the mid-tones show a well-defined gradation. The lines and wrinkles of the man's skin are enhanced by the use of black and white. One main light was used to the right with a fill-in light on the other side. A light above the head was used to illuminate the hair. The shot was taken on 100 ISO film.

● BELOW If you are in doubt as to whether a shot should be in colour or black and white and you have two cameras, shoot both as here. The black and white print was deliberately printed on a hard paper to bring out the contrast in the grass. Both shots were taken with the same wide angle lens within minutes of each other.

PROCESSING YOUR FILM

Once you have taken your photographs you will want to see the results as soon as possible. Many places now offer film processing and claim that they give a unique and professional service; but in fact often the film is collected and sent to a central processing laboratory. Here each film is given a computer identification code and they are all joined together in one huge reel like a movie film. The films are processed and printed in rapid succession, the prints cut up and put in wallets, and back everything goes to the shop where you handed in the film.

This sort of processing does not produce results of very good quality, nor is it consistent. If you send the same negative to be printed at the same laboratory several times, the chances are that each time it will come back with a different colour cast. In order to obtain the best results with expensive equipment, or when you have taken the greatest care in composing and exposing your pictures make sure the processing laboratory is a good one.

THE PROFESSIONAL WAY

A professional photographer, especially one who uses colour reversal film, has a close relationship with the technicians at his laboratory. The laboratory will maintain the highest standards, simply because if it does not, photographers will not use it any more.

A professional laboratory can clip test film: before the technicians process the whole film they will cut off the first few frames and process them. You can then check these and ask for adjustments to the rest of the batch. They can adjust the processing in increments of as little as $1/8$ of a stop (one stop is equivalent to the difference between f8 and f11, or between exposure times of $1/60$ and $1/125$ second).

Of course, for this to be worthwhile the film must be consistently exposed, and where the film is cut one or two frames will be lost. There is also a small extra charge for the clip test on top of the cost of processing the rest of the film. Kodachrome Professional film is bought with the processing paid for, but even this can now be clip tested and settings adjusted as necessary.

HOME PROCESSING

The more adventurous can buy home processing kits for both colour negative and colour reversal film, and also for black and white. You do not need to have a fully equipped darkroom to process film. Apart from the equipment in the kit all you need is a processing tank – these come in various sizes, depending on how many films you want to process at once – and a light-tight room or cupboard where you can load the film into the tank. Once this is done, the rest of the process is carried out in normal light, though of course you have to go back into the dark to make prints.

PUSHING AND PULLING

If a film is underexposed, for instance if it is uprated, it needs to be given a longer than normal development time. This is called 'pushing'. Overexposed film is 'pulled' by being developed for a shorter time than normal. These techniques are common, but they should not be used where they can be avoided because both of them cause a certain loss of picture quality: the harder a film has been pushed or pulled, the greater the loss. There is no substitute for getting your exposures spot on.

ENLARGED PRINTS

Again, a professional laboratory will give you substantially better enlarged prints. You will be able to discuss how you want your picture cropped and positioned on the masking frame of the enlarger. If a transparency that is to be printed has a colour cast you can ask for this to be corrected. You can even have particular areas of a negative or transparency shaded or printed up to darken or brighten them. This can be important if there is a large discrepancy between the tones in highlighted areas and shadows.

● Colour or black and white, transparency or negative – after you have taken your shots, good processing is essential.

WHAT THE APERTURE DOES

There are different sized apertures on a camera to allow different amounts of light to pass through onto the film. When the shutter is released it allows light to pass through the aperture. It is necessary to have a shutter as well as an aperture because the aperture controls depth of field as well as contributing to the exposure of a film.

The correlation between shutter speed and aperture size is a direct one; the immediate situation or the effect required dictates the necessary combination of shutter speed and size of aperture. If, for instance, an exposure of $\frac{1}{15}$ second and an aperture of f22 are needed, the aperture would get wider as the shutter speed increases

e.g. $\frac{1}{30}$ second   f16

         $\frac{1}{60}$ second   f11

         $\frac{1}{125}$ second   f8

DEPTH OF FIELD

The depth of field is the distance in front of and beyond the sharply focused subject of the picture. With a standard lens set on its widest aperture of f1.8, for example, and a subject 2 yards (1.8 m) from the camera, very little of the background and even less of the foreground would be in focus. However, if the lens is stopped down and the aperture is set to f16 or f22 much more of the background and foreground will be sharp.

With a wide angle lens depth of field will be greater even at wider apertures than it would be with a telephoto lens.

Depth of field plays an important part of the creation of a finished photograph. If, for example, the subject of the picture is a head and shoulders portrait of a person, yet with a distracting or unattractive background, it can be the depth of field that can be altered to put the background out of focus so that the person is the only clear part of the shot. If, on the other hand, the background is important or the subject is a group of people or objects at different distances from the camera where each one must appear sharp, a small aperture is needed. A small aperture would bring more of the picture into sharp focus.

AUTOMATIC CAMERAS

Some automatic cameras have a system called aperture priority. When the aperture is set the camera automatically adjusts the shutter speed. Care must be taken in cases where the chosen aperture is quite small, e.g. f11 or f16, as the shutter speed selected may be too slow to take an accurate shot without the steadying aid of a tripod or other support.

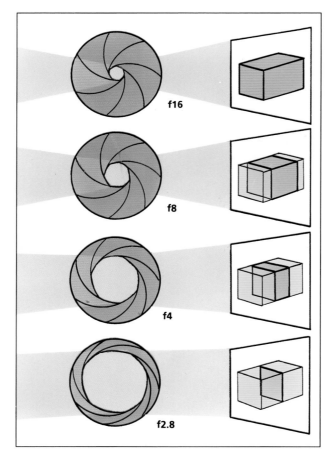

● LEFT There is a direct correlation between aperture size and depth of field. As the aperture decreases, more of the subject is in focus.

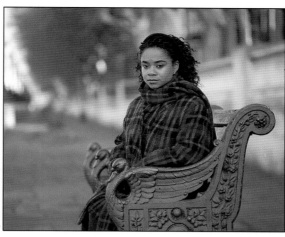

- This picture was taken using a standard lens at an aperture of f2.8. The girl is in focus and so is the front arm of the seat but everything else is out of focus.

- In this picture a medium telephoto lens was used and focused on the girl. Depth of field is minimal at an aperture of f4.5.

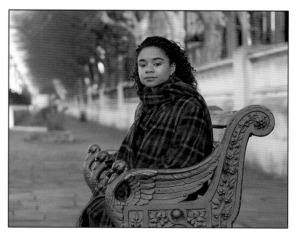

- In this picture an aperture of f8 was used. More of the seat and background are sharper but the distance is still unclear.

- Using the same telephoto lens an aperture of f11 has been used but the background still remains very soft.

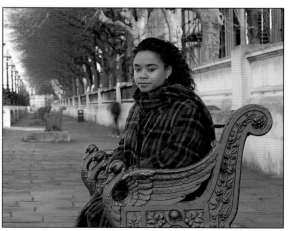

- Here the lens was stopped down to f22 and all the seat is sharp and the far distance is only slightly soft. By reducing the size of the aperture more of the picture is brought into focus i.e. the depth of field increases.

- With the lens stopped right down to f32 much more of the picture is in focus, yet it is not as sharp as in the first picture. Depth of field is greater with wide angle lenses than it is with telephoto lenses.

WHAT THE SHUTTER SPEED DOES

● BELOW A leaf shutter (top) and a focal plane shutter (below) in the process of opening.

EQUIPMENT & TECHNIQUES

The opening of the shutter of a camera determines the amount of time light is allowed to pass through the lens onto the film. As well as affecting exposure, the shutter speed can also freeze a moving object as a sharp image on film and reduce camera shake.

PORTRAYING FAST-MOVING OBJECTS

For hand-held shots it is virtually impossible to hold the camera completely steady at shutter speeds of 1/30 second or less without mounting the camera on a tripod or bracing it against a solid support, such as a wall.

Imagine a car or a person passing quickly across a chosen viewpoint. If the shutter speed is set at 1/60 second or less the moving object would appear blurred on the photograph. However, if the shutter speed were 1/250 second or more the moving object would be clear, 'frozen' in action. In the case of the car, it can be difficult to tell whether it is moving or stationary; this may result in a dull picture. A better way to illustrate action is to use a slower shutter speed and 'pan' the camera, following the moving object and taking the picture when it is directly in front. This type of photography may take a little practice to perfect but it produces striking images where the background is blurred and the moving object sharp, illustrating very effectively the speed at which it was travelling.

USING FLASH WITH SLR CAMERAS

With SLR cameras the shutter speed should be set to the manufacturers' recommended setting when using flash. This is usually 1/60 or 1/125 second. If a faster speed is used, only part of the film will be exposed as the flash will fire before the blinds of the shutter have

● LEFT Shutters at various stages of opening. TOP A leaf shutter. BOTTOM A focal plane shutter.

● BELOW When using flash with a camera that has a focal plane shutter it is important to set the camera at the manufacturer's designated speed. This might be $1/125$ second, for instance, or there might be a flash symbol on the shutter speed dial for this. If the speed used is in excess of this setting, only part of the frame will be exposed.

● BELOW LEFT In this picture the camera was mounted on a tripod and a slow shutter speed, $1/4$ second, was used.

● RIGHT When a long exposure is required, in this case 20 seconds, the shutter was set to the T setting. This meant that when the shutter was fired it remained open until it was depressed again. If the camera only has a setting on the shutter speed dial marked B, the shutter release has to remain depressed.

fully opened. With cameras that have a leaf shutter or a shutter between the lens the flash can be synchronized to any speed. This is a great advantage in situations where flash has to be balanced with daylight.

B AND *T* SETTINGS

On some shutter speed dials there are two settings marked B and T. When the shutter ring is set to B the shutter will remain open for as long as the shutter release button is depressed. If it is set to T, the shutter will remain open even when the shutter release button is released, closing when the button is depressed again. Both these settings are for use with pictures that require a long exposure.

*A*UTOMATIC *S*HUTTER *S*PEED *S*ELECTION

Some automatic cameras have metering modes called shutter priority. This means that when the shutter speed is adjusted manually the camera selects the aperture automatically.

● LEFT If the camera is moved in line with a moving object and a shutter speed of $1/60$ second is used, the object will remain sharp but the background will be blurred. This technique is called panning.

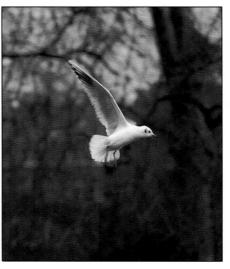

● LEFT By contrast, a shutter speed of $1/250$ second was used to photograph this bird in flight, and it has 'frozen' virtually all movement.

EQUIPMENT & TECHNIQUES

Most cameras today have built-in exposure metering systems. These should enable the photographer to get the correct exposure every time. However, in many situations the metering system is led astray by the general level of light, so that the subject of the photograph is over- or underexposed. This is because many systems take an average reading of the illumination over the whole frame. If you are photographing a person against a white wall, or if there is a lot of sky in the frame, these big light areas will have the greatest influence on the meter. Unless you compensate for this the person will come out underexposed, in extreme cases reduced to a silhouette. Conversely, if you place a person against a dark background the metering system will read mainly for this area, and if you do not make an adjustment the person will come out overexposed.

THE AUTOMATIC EXPOSURE LOCK

This problem can be resolved by using the camera's automatic exposure lock. This sets itself when the shutter release is lightly pressed. It holds the current exposure setting until the release is pressed to fire the shutter, or until the button is released altogether. So you can go up close to your subject, take an accurate reading from their flesh tones, hold down the shutter release and go back to your chosen viewpoint for the

● ABOVE Bracketing exposures lets you make slight variations in exposure that may make all the difference to the final picture. In this case the difference was ⅓ of a stop between each one. Here, TOP, the meter gave a reading that has slightly underexposed the girl, making her eyes look heavy and dark.

With the aperture increased slightly, MIDDLE, the skin tones are more natural and the shadowiness of the eyes has been eliminated.

A further increase in the exposure has made the facial features begin to burn out. So the picture on the BOTTOM would be chosen for the final print.

composition. If you want to take several shots you will have to follow the same procedure for each one.

SPOT METERING

If your camera has a variable metering system, you can use spot metering in such cases. This restricts the meter to measuring the light falling on a small spot in the centre of the viewfinder.

USING A HAND-HELD METER

There are two main ways of taking a reading with a hand-held meter:
● For a reflected light reading, point the meter at the subject and take a reading of the light reflected from it.
● For an incident light reading, place a small white disc, or invercone, over the meter cell. Some meters have a white blind which can be slid over the cell. Hold the meter against the subject and point it back towards the camera. This gives a more accurate reading of the light falling on the subject.

BRACKETING

Another way of getting the correct exposure is to bracket. For example, imagine that the metering system is giving a reading of ¹/₁₂₅ at f8. If you take one shot at this setting, one slightly over it and one slightly under, when the film is processed you can judge which exposure has worked best and make a print from that negative.

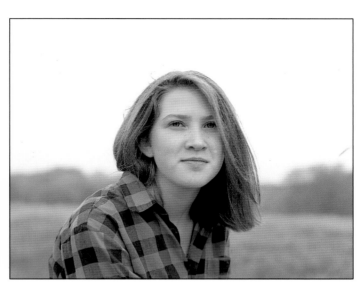

● ABOVE The camera meter took an average reading. As there was so much sky, which even on a dull day is bright in comparison to other areas of the picture, the girl has come out underexposed. ABOVE RIGHT Going in close and using the camera's exposure lock has given a truer reading of the flesh tones and a far more flattering exposure.

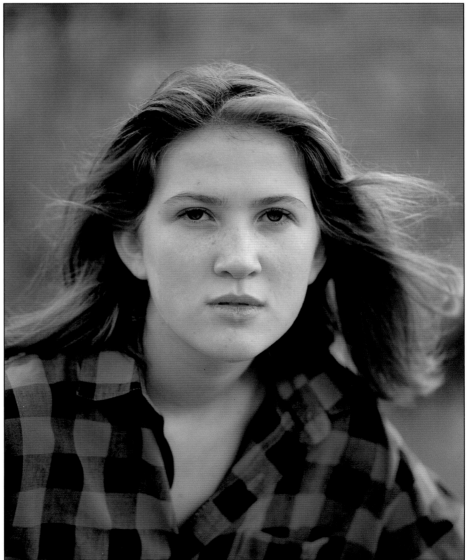

● RIGHT Spot metering has given an accurate exposure of the girl. If your camera does not have this feature you will have to use the exposure lock or a hand-held meter.

GENERAL COMPOSITION

Cameras are becoming increasingly sophisticated with their built-in exposure metering systems, and it would seem to follow that the photographer has more time to concentrate on areas such as composition. However, this is often not the case. Unwanted intrusions confuse and distract the eye; backgrounds that are irrelevant or dominating overpower the foreground, and foregrounds that should lead the eye into the picture either occupy too great an area or appear merely because of incorrect framing. All these faults can be corrected with very little effort and only minimal preparation.

● ABOVE Even when a photographic opportunity occurs by chance, it pays to take time to consider the general composition. Here the chess board fills the centre of the foreground and the two subjects are positioned on either side, creating a perfect balance. The scene captures a particular image of society, especially with the inclusion of the third man in the background; although not deliberately arranged, the three people and the juxtaposed chess board have become key elements in the final photograph.

● ABOVE This very simple shot has all the ingredients of a good composition. The foreground is uncluttered, and the pathway leads from the foreground directly to the centre of interest, the house. The house is set against a backdrop of small hills, which do not overpower the house but provide a contrast and add interest by breaking up the uniform stretch of blue sky.

● ABOVE This nutseller is the centre of interest and as such occupies the middle position in the shot. Do not be afraid of placing the subject in a prominent position within the frame of the picture. Here the subject sits among a display of his wares; this helps draw the eye towards him yet also around him as more and more items become apparent. Always retain an even balance between the subject and his surroundings.

● RIGHT The arch in the foreground provides a natural frame for this scene in a church in Moscow. This arch is complemented by a series of other arches that can be seen in the background as the eye travels from one to the other in a smooth sequence. There are no unsightly intrusions in either the foreground or background. This is a strong composition which may well have been weaker if taken from a different viewpoint.

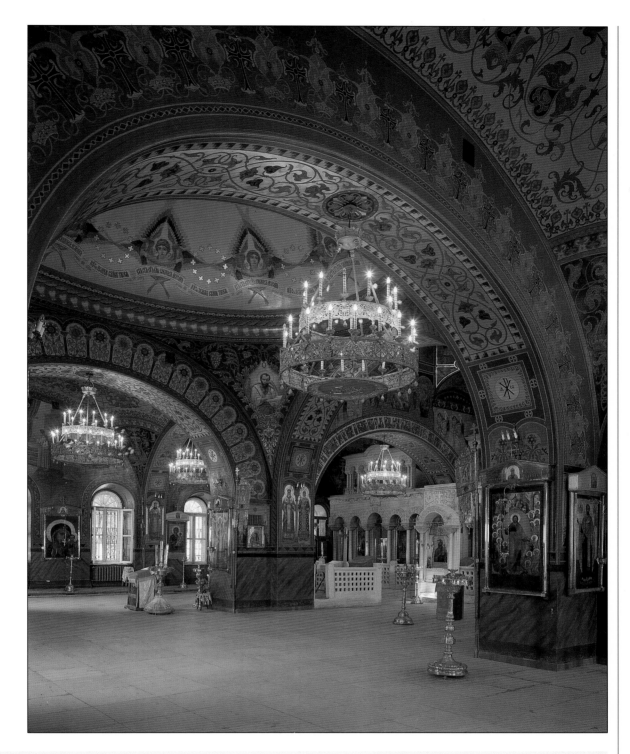

THREE KEY AREAS TO BE CONSIDERED IN COMPOSITION:

1 The centre of interest – having decided what the central subject of the photograph is to be, ascertain where the photograph is to be shot from to achieve the most effective background.

2 Possible distractions or intrusions – examine carefully the subject, background and foreground to ensure the picture will not be spoilt by an unwanted object. It is only too easy to mar a beautiful building with a traffic sign in the foreground, or to produce a portrait of some friends complete with a telegraph pole emerging from the top of one of their heads. Usually an intruding object can be removed from the composition simply by moving slightly to one side. It is worth waiting for any moving vehicles to pass by.

3 Enhancing the foreground – it is important to decide if there is anything that might add to the foreground without detracting from or obscuring the centre of interest.

USING FOREGROUND

Foregrounds can play an important part in the general composition of photographs. A point of interest in the foreground close to the camera can be used either as a framing device or as a tool to lead the eye into the picture. This type of added interest can make all the difference between the exciting and the mediocre.

USING FOREGROUND AS A DISGUISE

Foregrounds can also be used to hide untidy objects or unwanted intrusions in the middle or background of the picture. However, it is important to make sure that the foreground does not dominate the picture as then it will detract from the main subject of the photograph, becoming as much of an intrusion as the detail it is attempting to disguise.

OBJECTS IN THE FOREGROUND

Although objects in the foreground of a picture can add interest, it is all too easy to let them appear with monotonous regularity. This is a danger with a series of pictures taken from similar viewpoints, yet can be easily avoided with a little thought. Take time to evaluate what is in front of the camera; use all the components to their best advantage in the final shot.

When objects are included in the foreground care must be taken with the exposure. Check to see if the objects are in shadow compared to the central portion of the shot and background as this may produce an ugly dark shape with no detail visible. If the shadow is unavoidable try correcting it using a reflector or fill-in flash.

Also check to see if the camera needs to be higher than the object in the foreground. If not, make sure the object is not filling too much of the frame.

● LEFT This picture of a formal garden has been enhanced by the use of the foliage of the outer trees as a framing device. The gates at the bottom of the frame complete the foreground interest. The result gives the impression of peering into a 'secret' garden. If the camera had been positioned further forward and the foreground lost, the picture would have looked entirely different.

USE OF PERSPECTIVE TO CREATE FOREGROUND INTEREST

Additional foreground interest can be created by the use of perspective, for example the furrows in a ploughed field stretching out into the distance. In this case, a low viewpoint might be best. When taking a landscape shot the sky can often be a dominating factor so that the landscape scene itself is overpowered. If this happens, perhaps the addition of a tree with overhanging branches within the shot could frame the top of the picture and diminish the impact of the sky.

● ABOVE Foreground objects do not always need to be placed dead centre. Here the boat is in the bottom right-hand corner of the frame and creates an added degree of foreground interest. The colour of the boat complements the colour of the lush green grass without providing too harsh a contrast. If a picture of this sort is to be part of a series, try to vary the position of the object in the foreground so that it does not become a dull motif, detracting from the shots themselves.

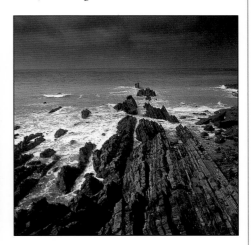

● ABOVE The strong lines of the strata shoot out from the foreground and pierce the sea, leading the eye straight into the picture and creating a powerful composition. If the photograph had been taken from a position at the end of the rocks, the foreground would have been merely a dull stretch of sea with no added interest.

● ABOVE Not all historical buildings are always at their best – as here in Reims, France, where the cathedral was covered in scaffolding. Added to this the early-morning sun rose behind the cathedral and since there was no time to wait for the sun's position to alter a viewpoint was found some distance from the front of the building. A telephoto lens, 200 mm, was used and by having as a framing device the trees in the foreground the untidy scaffolding was concealed and the direct sunlight was blocked.

USING BACKGROUND

The background of a picture can enhance the overall composition of an image in ways similar to the effects of the foreground. As a general rule, backgrounds should not dominate the photograph, obscuring the main subject. This jars the eye and gives an overall impression of a cluttered photograph. Similarly, a flat, dull background can influence the whole picture so that all interest is lost. A telephoto lens can produce a compressed image, bringing the background forward and reducing the depth between the middle- and foreground.

The weather can create dramatic effects; if dark clouds are hanging in the sky watch out for isolated bursts of sunlight which can spotlight areas of the foreground, underexposing and making the dark areas even darker.

When taking a shot of an apparently tranquil landscape, check to see if there are any roads or tracks running through. If there are, wait until traffic has dispersed as an unsightly track can ruin an otherwise beautiful scene.

● ABOVE LEFT The cows form an almost monochromatic background to this picture. The track that comes down to the gate balances the picture and enhances the general composition, yet nothing detracts from the young girl. Her bright raincoat and hat are set off by the black and white cows, and the juxtaposition of her diminutive size alongside the cows adds a subtle touch of humour to the shot.

● ABOVE RIGHT The ever-burning flame of this oil refinery on the banks of the Mississippi at New Orleans relieves an otherwise dull background. It also provides a powerful contrast with the more traditional technology of the old paddle steamer in the foreground. It always pays to be alert to pictures where the back- and foregrounds provide not only a visual contrast but can also make a wider abstract statement in visual terms.

● RIGHT This picture was taken using only the available light coming in through a small window and with an exposure of 1/8 second, bracing the camera against the bar. It is a clear example of how the background can provide information about the subject while at the same time adding extra interest and detail.

● LEFT This salmon fisherman is holding a putcher, a funnel-shaped basket used to catch salmon as they swim out to sea. The stakes stretching out behind echo the mood of the putcher, and convey a greater sense of the man and his work.

KEY POINTS TO NOTE ABOUT BACKGROUNDS:

1 Is the background overpowering? Will it overshadow the subject of the picture? On the other hand, does it have enough interest to prevent it from being dull?

2 Does the background behind a human subject represent anything about the person's work or environment?

3 Are the background colours harmonious or unusual in some way? A telephoto lens can push the background out of focus, throwing up some interesting shapes and muted colours.

4 Does the sky appear in the background? If there are any clouds, try to retain their clarity and detail, perhaps by using a graduated neutral density filter or polarizing filter, or a yellow filter with black and white film.

CHOOSING A VIEWPOINT

There are many situations when taking a photograph where a simple alteration of viewpoint can make all the difference. Viewpoint can be defined as the position from which a photograph is taken, and takes into account the background and foreground, and any interesting angles that will lead the eye naturally towards the emphasis of the image. By using different viewpoints the photographer can dramatically alter the impact of a picture.

Often people will say to a professional photographer something along the lines of, 'But you've got all the equipment!' In fact, all that it takes to achieve a better view is a little thought of where one should stand and how the foreground can be utilized to the greatest effect. On many occasions it may be possible to utilize detail in the foreground by either tilting the camera downward or by moving slightly to one side. These small shifts of position or angle, that may seem insignificant at the time, can produce the difference between the dramatic and the dull.

● BELOW The choice of lens is important for the composition of a picture.

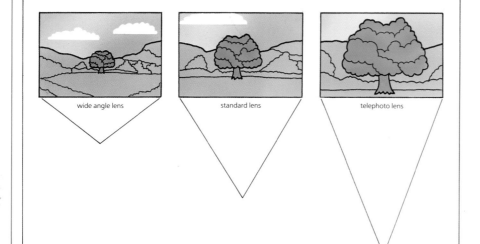

wide angle lens   standard lens   telephoto lens

● ABOVE AND INSET Viewed individually there may seem little to choose between these two pictures of Brooklyn Bridge. The shots were taken within 46 m (150 ft) of one another and within a short space of time. The upper picture was taken from further away than the lower one; much of its impact is lost by the inclusion of too much sky at the top of the frame, and the cloud is an added distraction.

The lower picture was taken from much nearer to the bridge using a slightly lower viewpoint. This means that the verticals have converged to a greater degree than they would have done had the shot been taken from a higher position, and the tension cables fill the frame, fanning out in all directions to draw the eye into the shot. The cloud has been cropped out which extends the symmetry of the shot; with fewer distractions the graphic qualities of the composition are enhanced.

EASY ESTIMATING

To help judge your choice of viewpoint, simply form a rectangle between the thumbs and forefingers of both hands, and look through to judge your chosen image.

To tighten the 'frame', slide the right hand closer to the left, keeping the rectangle steady. In order to create a 'zoom' effect, extend your arms so that the background is removed and the

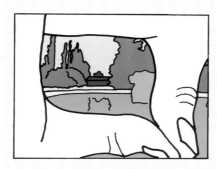

subject of the picture appears larger in relation to the rectangle.

● ABOVE Standing close to one element of a photograph can add extra emphasis. The viewpoint for this picture was created by standing close to the canyon wall that appears on the left. The dramatic sweep of the wall and its horizontal strata lead the eye straight into the picture. If taken from a different position or angle the effect would have been weaker.

● RIGHT By tilting the camera downward the lilies on the water are brought into the picture. This provides extra interest in the foreground without detracting from the mountains and sky beyond. If the camera had been horizontal or tilted upward slightly, without including the lilies, the result would have been a rather dull stretch of water and reflected cloud in the foreground.

Daylight colour film, as its name suggests, is for use with daylight-lit subjects or with electronic flash. If daylight film is used indoors where the main source of illumination is provided by domestic light bulbs, the resulting pictures will have a predominantly orange cast to them. This is because what is known as the 'colour temperature' of the light source would be at variance with the colour balance of the film.

COLOUR TEMPERATURE

Colour temperature is usually measured in values of kelvin. To achieve the correct balance when using daylight film in artificial light of 3200 kelvin requires the use of an 80A filter. This is a blue-coloured filter which corrects the orange cast that is otherwise created. However, the blue-coloured filter is quite a dense filter and will cut down the amount of light passing through the lens onto the film; to compensate for this, 64 ISO film must be rated at 16 ISO. Care must be taken when adjusting for these factors as a long exposure is needed — yet most daylight-balanced colour film suffers from reciprocity failure at exposures of 1 second or longer.

When you expose daylight-balanced colour film for exposures of longer than approximately 1 second, the film will suffer from reciprocity failure i.e. where the stated ISO rating no longer applies. An example of this is where a 100 ISO film may only be 25 ISO at an exposure of 10 seconds. Owing to the unpredictable nature of the film in these circumstances, the only sure way of getting the right exposure is to test the film in the prevailing light conditions to see what ISO it should be rated at.

When using tungsten-balanced colour reversal films and the few tungsten-balanced colour negative films available these problems are solved. There is no need to add a filter to the camera when shooting in situations where the colour temperature is 3200 kelvin, and tungsten-balanced film can be used at far longer exposures than daylight film without suffering from reciprocity failure.

If daylight-balanced colour negative film is used in tungsten light it can always be corrected at printing stage. If daylight-balanced colour reversal film is used in tungsten light without an 80A filter the resulting transparencies would have to be duplicated and corrected at the printing stage. This is expensive, and, however good the duplicates are, some of the quality will inevitably be lost.

● TOP LEFT If daylight-balanced colour film is used in artificial light the results will have an orange cast. To correct this imbalance an 80A filter needs to be used, TOP RIGHT. Alternatively, tungsten-balanced film used in artificial light does not require a colour-balanced filter.

● BOTTOM LEFT Using tungsten film in daylight or with electronic flash will result in pictures with a blue cast. To correct this, use an 85B filter, BOTTOM RIGHT. As an alternative, use daylight-balanced film in daylight or with electronic flash as this does not need a colour-balanced filter.

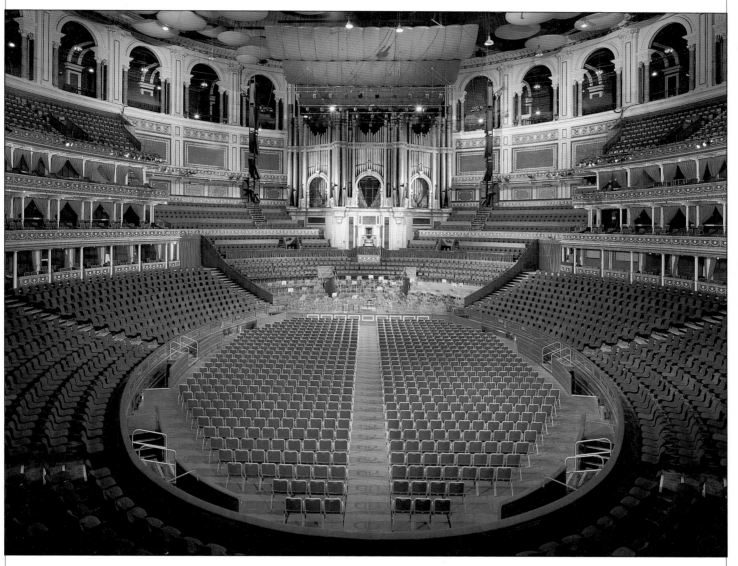

● ABOVE When shooting in artificial light it is often necessary to use long exposures. This picture required the shutter to be open for 30 seconds. Since the lighting was tungsten, tungsten-balanced colour film was used. Apart from the fact that it rendered the colour correctly, tungsten film suffers far less from reciprocity failure than daylight-balanced film.

average tungsten light   average daylight

2000		2500	2850		4000	5000	6000	10 000	20 000
500		400	350		250	200	160	100	50

● LEFT Light is measured in values of kelvin. The measurements change according to the type of light, from warm to cool.

Occasionally there are situations, especially indoors, when the light comes from many different light sources. These light sources may all have different colour temperatures, so using just tungsten-balanced film or filtering daylight-balanced film to 3200 kelvin may not be adequate.

FLUORESCENT LIGHT

One of the most difficult lights to balance is fluorescent light. This is because there are many different types of fluorescent light tubes ranging from cool to warm white. When a tube wears out it might be replaced with a tube of a different colour temperature. To the naked eye, all the tubes may look the same yet they are in fact giving off different temperatures of colour which makes choosing the correct filter very difficult.

DAYLIGHT MIXED WITH ARTIFICIAL LIGHT

Sometimes with two different light sources, such as tungsten light and daylight or fluorescent light and daylight, the only practical solution may be to expose for the greater light source. A more elaborate method – when shooting in a room lit by tungsten light with windows that let in daylight – is to place light-balancing material over the windows to convert the daylight to the same balance as the tungsten light.

In mixed light situations that combine daylight with tungsten, the warmth of the tungsten light can add a mellow tone. If the situation is one which combines daylight, tungsten and flash, the trick is to make all of these elements balance. The best method to achieve this is to work out the exposure for the daylight coming in through the windows. For example, it may be 1 second at f16. If so, adjust the power of the flash to give an exposure of f16. (Shooting at speeds slower than the flash setting on the camera will not alter the flash exposure; this will only happen if a faster speed is used than is recommended for the camera.) Set the shutter speed to 1 second and take the shot. At this exposure tungsten light (coming, for example, from a table lamp) will be recorded without causing an unnatural colour cast.

● ABOVE In the TOP shot daylight predominates and the picture comes out well on the daylight film in the camera. BOTTOM, using the same film and pointing the camera down to a small area of the building lit by tungsten light without the use of an 80A filter has created a definite orange cast.

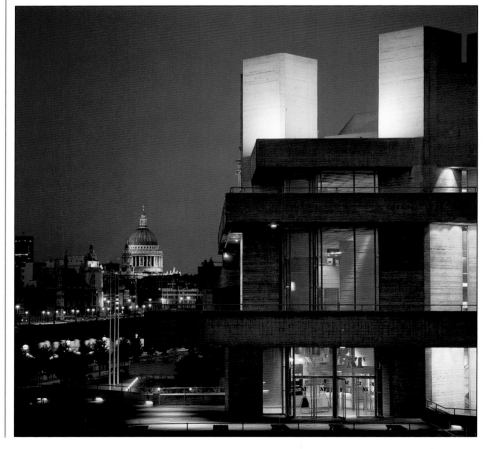

● LEFT This picture, taken outdoors at dusk, shows several different light sources but because of the expanse of the picture and its varied elements it appears correctly exposed even though the lights have differing colour balances.

● ABOVE This picture of the famous food halls of Harrods in London is a good example of a mixed light situation: the ceramic well set into the ceiling is lit by fluorescent lighting yet the rest of the store is lit by tungsten. In the time available it was impossible to put colour correction gels over all the fluorescent tubes so a compromise had to be reached. Since the fluorescent light was illuminating an isolated area, the whole shot was exposed for tungsten.

● FAR LEFT This museum room has fluorescent light as the dominant source which has given the shot a green cast. LEFT An FLD (fluorescent daylight) filter removes this and adds a natural tone.

Flash has become as commonplace as the cameras that use it. It provides a convenient, renewable, instant and often adjustable extra light source. Some cameras have built-in flash while other models take flash unit attachments. Professional photographers use large free-standing flash units for studio work yet excellent results can be obtained with less expensive equipment.

BUILT-IN FLASH

Built-in flash is very convenient, yet like any piece of equipment it has its drawbacks. The flash tends to be rather weak and any subject beyond approximately 10 ft (3 m) will be underexposed. The output of the flash may be constant and no adjustment available; the disadvantage of this is that anything very close to the flash will be burnt out. The most common problem is that of 'red eye'. 'Red eye' occurs when the flash is fired near the axis of the lens. If a shot is taken of a person looking at the camera, the flash will bounce off the retina of the eye and produce a red spot in the final picture. The remedy is to move the flash away from the axis of the lens. This cannot be done with built-in flash. If the flash is of the type that flashes several times in quick succession when the shutter release button is depressed, finally firing at full strength, the pupil of the eye contracts so that there is less of the retina from which the flash can be reflected and it does not appear red.

SEPARATE FLASH UNITS

Separate flash units may be more powerful than built-in flash. They are attached to the camera hot shoe or to a special bracket and sync lead. Many units have heads that can be angled upwards to varying degrees so that the light can be bounced off a ceiling or

● TOP LEFT Using a flash gun attached to the side of the camera creates a harsh light with a shadow to one side.

● BOTTOM LEFT Placing a diffuser over the flash softens the shadow but it is still quite obvious.

● TOP RIGHT By moving the flash even further to one side the shadow is accentuated.

● BOTTOM RIGHT By bouncing the light off the ceiling the shadow on the wall has been eliminated, but at the expense of a shadow under the chin.

other pale material. If this type of
angled flash is used for a portrait the
light will be softer but might result in
dark shadows under the eyes, nose and
chin. These can be avoided by using
fill-in flash.

FILL-IN FLASH

A built-in fill-in flash unit is positioned
under the main flash attachment.
When the flash is fired on 'bounce
mode' with the fill-in flash, 80 per cent
of the power passes through the main
flash while the remaining 20 per cent
goes through the fill-in unit. This
removes most of the shadows from under
the eyes, nose and chin. Another method
of softening flash light is to diffuse it.
This can be done very simply by placing
a small cloth such as a handkerchief
over the flash, or even by holding a
piece of tracing paper just in front of
the flash itself.

● TOP LEFT
Sometimes daylight is
not enough even
though a built-in
meter may advise you
to the contrary.

● BOTTOM LEFT Fill-
in balanced flash helps
eliminate the problem
by bringing the
exposure required for
the person to the same
level as that required
for the background.

● BELOW When the flash is directly in line with
the lens, a bleached-out face often results. There
is always the chance of 'red eye' as well.

● LEFT By bouncing the flash in this picture and
using a fill-in flash as well a more acceptable
picture is achieved.

USING WIDE ANGLE LENSES

EQUIPMENT & TECHNIQUES

Additional lenses are the accessories that will probably do the most to improve your photography. A wide angle lens offers you a completely different perspective on a traditional view. Not only will its wider angle of view get more into the picture, but it also has a greater depth of field than a normal or telephoto lens, so that more of the shot will be sharp.

You can have an object relatively close to the lens and still keep the background in focus. If the object is close enough it will look much larger in proportion to the rest of the picture than it really is. With extreme wide angle lenses, distortion can be a problem and you should not photograph people from too close in, to avoid unflattering results. For instance, a 21 mm lens pointed directly at someone's face will make the nose look enormous, the cheeks puffed out, and the ears as if they have moved round towards the back of their head. This might be fun at first, but the novelty will soon wear off and it will be time to turn to more serious applications.

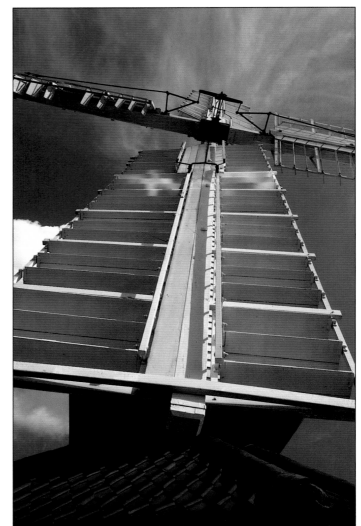

● ABOVE The impact of this shot relies on the feeling of the 'big' landscape. The wide field of view gives a feeling of overwhelming space and loneliness. The lines marked on the road exaggerate the already strong perspective and give the impression that the road goes on endlessly.

● RIGHT Using a low viewpoint with a wide angle lens makes it look as if the windmill sails are soaring into the sky. The great depth of field offered by the lens makes the whole picture sharp even though the bottom of the sail is quite close to the lens. It is very important to choose the correct viewpoint when using a lens of this kind.

● LEFT A drought has dried up this lake, exposing an old tree stump. Again, the wide angle lens keeps the whole picture sharp. Placing the stump at one side of the frame gives it an almost living quality, as if it is walking towards what remains of the lake.

● RIGHT When photographing people, take great care to avoid unflattering distortion. In this picture, although the hands and arms are distorted this is within tolerable limits and does not unbalance the composition as the viewpoint and angle of the shot have been carefully chosen. Although the arms look long and the hands, which are closest to the lens, enormous, the imbalance is acceptable because the strong hands represent the nature of the fisherman's work. His arms lead the eye straight to his face, which is framed in turn by a backdrop of his working environment. The busy background keeps the eye from dwelling too long on his hands so that, large as they are, they simply appear to be part of the composition.

USING TELEPHOTO LENSES

Telephoto lenses do much more than just bring distant objects closer. They can greatly enhance general composition. Their shallow depth of field can blur the background in a portrait to isolate and emphasize the subject. In contrast to wide angle lenses, going in close to people has a positively flattering effect. This is because a telephoto lens slightly compresses the picture so that prominent features such as the nose and ears stay in proportion. Careful use of a telephoto lens can also help to cut out unwanted foreground clutter, allowing you to get to the heart of the picture.

EXPOSURE AND APERTURE SETTINGS

Some compensation has to be made in settings when using a telephoto lens,
especially a long one. This is because the magnifying effect of the lens spreads the available light out more thinly, and the longer the lens the greater the effect. With cameras that have TTL metering this is no problem, but a manual camera will have to be adjusted.

Telephoto lenses also tend to have smaller apertures than normal or wide angle lenses, so that exposure must be longer. There are exceptions: some of the latest telephoto lenses have apertures as big as f2.8, but these lenses are very expensive, and few amateur photographers will consider that their usefulness justifies the price. If you need a fast long lens for a particular shot it would be more sensible to hire one.

USING A TRIPOD

The image made by a telephoto lens
shifts very rapidly when the camera is moved. This fact together with the long exposure time may call for the use of a tripod or monopod. With a lens over 300 mm this will be essential: it is almost impossible to hold the camera still enough to avoid shake and a blurred image.

CONVERTERS

You would need to use a very long lens such as a 500 mm very often to justify its high price. If not, you might consider using a converter. This fits between the camera body and an existing lens. A 2 x converter will increase the focal length of a 250 mm lens to 500 mm. The price is reasonable and the image almost as sharp as that of a long lens. Most camera manufacturers make converters.

● This was shot with a 28 mm wide angle lens. It has stretched the telephone boxes apart and given a very elongated effect.

● Here a 135 mm telephoto lens has been used. It has compressed the boxes so that they look closer together. The composition is far tighter and cuts out much unwanted detail from the frame.

● RIGHT The use of a 200 mm telephoto lens has cropped a lot of clutter out of the picture. The lens has compressed the picture, reducing the apparent space between buildings. Such a composition emphasizes the contrasts between the various architectural styles, from the Victorian classical façade to the modern skyscrapers in the background.

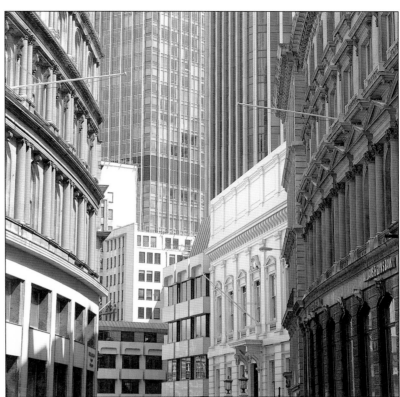

● BELOW A 100 mm telephoto lens is ideal for portraiture. Its short depth of field, especially at wide apertures, can put the background out of focus and thus allow the viewer to concentrate on the main subject. In such shots it is best to focus on the eyes and expose for the skin tones.

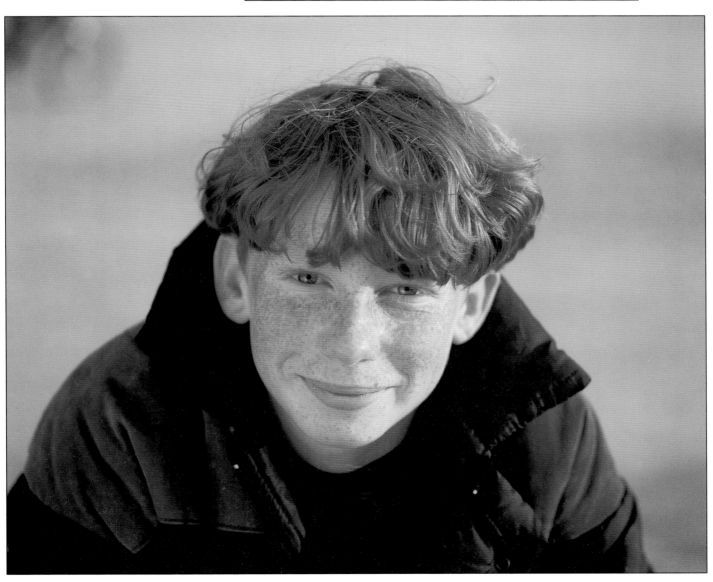

SHIFT LENSES

A shift lens, also called a perspective control (PC) lens, is a great addition to the photographer's equipment, and especially useful for architectural photography. With a 5 × 4 camera it is possible to move the front panel, on which the lens is mounted, up and down and from side to side, or to swing it vertically or tilt it horizontally. For 35 mm SLR and some medium format cameras there are lenses that can be moved up and down or across, and some lenses have a tilt facility as well. In the 35 mm range these lenses usually have a focal length of 28 or 35 mm.

When using one of these lenses to photograph a tall building, instead of tilting the camera up to fit in the whole building, the camera can be kept pointing straight ahead and the axis of the lens is shifted relative to the film plane — that is, the lens is moved upward but kept parallel to the film. This movement is known as a shift. The whole building now appears in the picture, but with a difference. With a normal lens and the camera angled up, the vertical lines of the building will converge towards the top of the frame. With a shift lens, as long as the camera is kept horizontal, all verticals in the picture will appear vertical and there will be no convergence, even when the lens is shifted as far as it can go.

Even when photographing things that are less strongly vertical, distortion can still be caused by angling the camera to cut out unwanted features such as an untidy foreground. Here, keeping the camera level and using a shift lens can eliminate unwanted areas at the bottom, top, left or right of the frame without causing distortion.

Before deciding to buy a shift lens, it is a good idea to hire one from a professional photography store and try out its effects.

● ABOVE To keep all the columns vertical in this shot of the Banqueting House in London, the camera had to be kept level. With a normal lens this would have cut out the wonderful ceiling painted by Rubens, and would have included a lot of the comparatively dull floor. Using the shift lens to its maximum has cut out much of the floor and brought in the ceiling.

● RIGHT A problem with photographing objects with shiny reflective surfaces, such as cars, is that the camera and photographer can appear in them. The effect can be corrected by standing to one side of the car, but by using the horizontal shift movement of the lens the car can be brought into the centre of the frame without the photographer or the camera appearing as a reflection.

- Using a conventional lens, the camera had to be tilted upward to fit the whole building into the frame. The vertical lines converge so that the building seems to be leaning.

- To keep the verticals straight the plane of the film must be parallel to the plane of the front of the building, which means that the camera body must be absolutely level. But here this results in the top of the tallest building being cut off.

- Here the camera is still level, but the shift lens has been moved upward. The whole building is now in view, but its sides are completely vertical. Also, a lot of uninteresting foreground detail has been cropped out of the picture.

FISHEYE LENSES

Among all the lenses that are available the fisheye lens is low on most people's list of priorities. The uses of this lens are limited and it is rather expensive. Nevertheless, it can be highly effective in the right situation.

It is sensible to hire a fisheye lens from a professional photographic dealer and try it out before deciding to buy one. If there seem to be many genuinely worthwhile uses for it, then and only then consider a purchase.

Most people looking through an SLR camera with a fisheye lens for the first time find it highly amusing to see the world through a 180-degree angle of vision. Objects appear severely distorted, and it is easy to get carried away by gimmicky shots of people's faces close to the lens, but used thoughtfully, a fisheye lens can produce uniquely striking images. The art of exploiting the lens is to make the photograph look as if a fisheye lens has not been used at all. Great care is needed in choosing a viewpoint and in framing the subject to obtain the best effect.

Because of their extremely wide angle of view, fisheye lenses cannot be used with lens hoods. Filters can be fitted, but these are special ones that are screwed in at the back of the lens. Graduated filters cannot be used.

There is a difficulty when using flash. Even when a flash gun is fitted with a wide angle attachment, the area that it illuminates is no wider than the field of view of a 28 mm lens. This falls far short of what is needed for a fisheye. If flash has to be used, at least two, even three or four flash heads are needed.

● ABOVE This hallway ceiling needed to be lit with flash, and four flash heads were necessary to give the required coverage. The symmetry of the design has created an interesting architectural conundrum.

● BELOW Like the domed British Museum Reading Room, the Olympic cycle track in Moscow lends itself well to being photographed with a fisheye lens. The banked curves at both ends look much as might be expected, and not unduly distorted. The ceiling panels add to a strong feeling of perspective.

● ABOVE A good example of how to use a fisheye lens without the result looking gimmicky. The Reading Room of the British Museum has a domed ceiling and the reading desks radiate out from the centre of the floor. Keeping the camera level allows the beautiful dome to be seen in its entirety, as well as including the floor in the shot. The curved lines of the room harmonize with the distortion caused by the lens, so that the shot looks as if it had been taken with a normal wide angle lens.

● LEFT Taken from the dome of the cathedral in Florence, Italy, this fisheye shot gives a striking panoramic view. The inclusion of the dome itself in the foreground leads the eye into the maze of streets below, and out into the Tuscan countryside beyond.

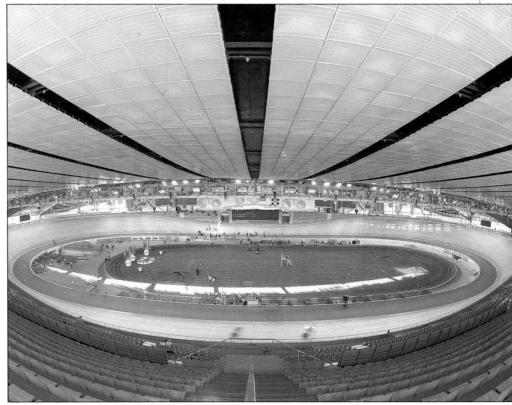

EQUIPMENT & TECHNIQUES

Zoom lenses allow the use of a continuous range of focal lengths without having to change lenses. If two zoom lenses are used, it is possible with only one change to go from 28 mm wide angle to 300 mm telephoto. The image quality is not quite as good as that of a prime lens, but the slight difference will be apparent only to the most critical viewer.

Many zoom lenses can now be used with autofocus systems, but some of these cannot take certain filter holders. It is as well to make sure what will fit before a problem arises.

As well as taking conventional pictures at any chosen focal length, a zoom lens can also be 'zoomed' during the exposure to create an interesting effect. This should be done during a moderately long exposure, say $\frac{1}{8}$ second, to make the movement apparent. There will be a pattern of streaks radiating from the centre of the frame. Zooming from wide angle to telephoto will create a different effect from going the other way. The most effective shots with this technique are those which have strong highlights or colours which will make a noticeable pattern. This gives a feeling of movement, as if the objects are flying straight out of the frame. The slow shutter speed will require the camera to be mounted on a tripod. It may take a little practice to perfect the technique, but passable results should be achieved quite quickly. Like all special effects, this should not be over-used.

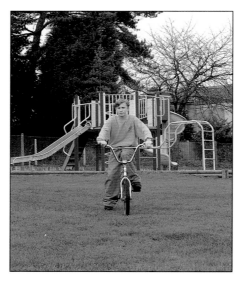

● ABOVE Here is a conventional view of a boy standing astride his bike. He is deliberately placed in front of a strongly coloured backdrop.

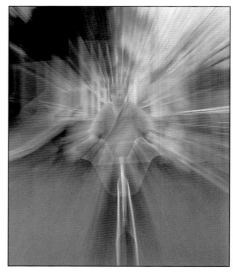

● ABOVE Here, he is in the same position, but this time a shutter speed of $\frac{1}{8}$ second was chosen, and during the exposure the lens was zoomed half-way through its range of focal length. This created strong radiating lines of colour and gives a sense of speed.

● RIGHT The boy is still in the same position, but the lens has been moved from 80 mm to 300 mm. It looks as if he is going round a corner at speed.

● **ABOVE** Neon lights make a good subject for zooming. Here is the conventional view . . .

● **LEFT** . . . and here is the effect with the zoom.

Additional equipment may not be absolutely necessary, but it can offer new photographic possibilities. One of the most useful accessories is some means of taking close-up shots. There are several ways of doing this.

The cheapest is a close-up lens which is fitted over the normal camera lens. This does not, however, give a very high-quality image. When using such a lens on an SLR camera, focusing and framing are relatively easy, but when it is fitted to a camera with a viewfinder the distance to the subject must be measured. The lens will come with instructions about the correction to make to the focus setting. Because the viewfinder is offset, an educated guess will have to be made about how to point the camera.

For some SLR cameras it is possible to buy a reversing ring. This allows the lens to be mounted back to front, which makes it possible to focus on closer objects. The lens is not designed to be used backwards, so the image will not be of the best quality.

The only really satisfactory methods are to use extension rings or bellows, or to buy a separate macro lens. The rings or bellows are fixed to the camera as a lens would be, and the lens is attached to the front. Extension rings usually come in sets of three, and can be used singly or together. When using them with certain lenses 1:1 magnification can be obtained, which means that the image is the same size as the object. Bellows work in the same way, but can be moved smoothly in and out so that any degree of magnification within their range can be obtained.

A macro lens allows close-up work without having to fuss with these awkward devices. However, some macro lenses can be used with rings or bellows to give even greater magnification.

● ABOVE The two small leaves were photographed with a macro lens and extension rings. The magnification on the original film was 1:1, life-size. A soft focus filter was used on the lens and the leaves were lit by electronic flash with a very soft diffuser. When working at such high magnifications exposure time has to be increased considerably.

● LEFT This picture was taken with a macro lens at almost full magnification. A problem with any close-up work is depth of field, which at very high magnification is almost non-existent, as the picture shows. The nails are 6 cm (2½ in) long and quite thin, but when they are perfectly in focus the background, a mere 3 mm (⅛ in) away, is blurred.

● BELOW The section of lemon was photographed on a blue plate. The glaze is out of focus even though a tiny aperture of f45 was used, because the depth of field is so shallow. The high magnification and small aperture called for a very long exposure. The camera will always need to be mounted on a tripod, and it is advisable to use a cable release. If the camera has a mirror-up facility, operate this before firing the shutter, since even the slightest vibration caused by the mirror may blur the picture. It is also vital to make sure that the subject stays still.

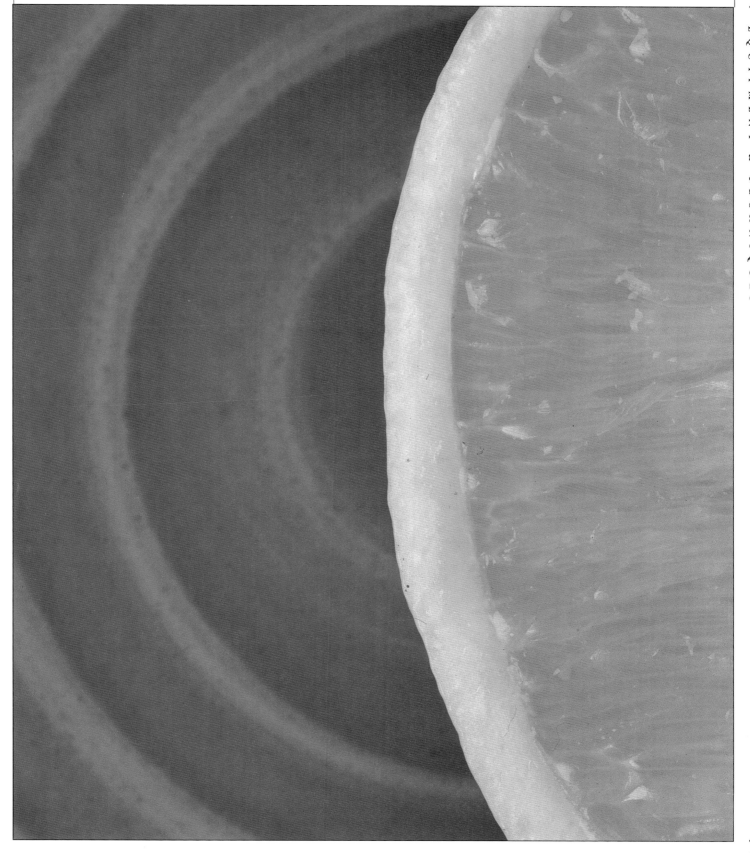

EQUIPMENT & TECHNIQUES

Of all the accessories that are available, filters are the cheapest. Yet these simple attachments to the front of the lens – or sometimes to the rear – can radically alter the effect of a picture. There is a myriad of types to choose from. As with any camera accessory, you must pay attention to a few points in order to get a satisfying result.

Some filters cut down the amount of light entering the lens to such an extent that a longer exposure is needed. If your camera has TTL metering this will not be a problem, but with other cameras you will have to adjust exposure manually. Manufacturers of filters generally state the necessary amount of exposure adjustment: this is called the filter factor.

With a wide angle lens, vignetting may occur when a filter is put in front of the lens. This means that the corners of the frame are cut off, because the angle of view of the lens is so great that it takes in the filter holder ring. This usually happens only with lenses of 21 mm or wider.

It is possible to use more than one filter at a time, but do this only if it will enhance the image.

Some special effect filters, such as multiple image types, are fun but their use is strictly limited. Imagine looking at your holiday photographs and seeing them all as if through a kaleidoscope. You would quickly get bored. Even a graduated tobacco filter, which can help to lift a dull sky, would be tedious if all your pictures had this coloured sky.

● ABOVE A multiple image filter makes several tiger's heads appear. These filters come in different types, such as 2, 4 or 6 images. They can be used creatively but not too often.

● BELOW LEFT No filter has been used. BELOW RIGHT A soft focus filter has been added to diffuse the image.

● LEFT When this shot of Venice was taken the sky was rather grey and flat. A graduated tobacco filter has changed the colour of the sky, but the rest of the picture is unaffected. This is an effective filter but use it sparingly, or all your shots will look too alike.

● ABOVE An alternative to the tobacco filter is this pink graduated filter. Although this shot was taken at midday the filter, carefully used, makes it look like dawn.

● RIGHT A graduated neutral density filter will darken a sky without changing the colour. In this shot of Loch Torridon it has turned an already moody sky to a virtually night-time hue.

Often a photograph can be greatly enhanced by the use of a reflector or what is called fill-in flash. To many people it seems odd that you would use flash in bright sunlight but it helps by reducing unattractive shadows. Suppose it is a bright day and the sun is quite high. Imagine that the people you are going to photograph are facing the sun. This will cause them to have dark shadows under their eyes and nose. Even if they turn to one side the shadows might still remain, or if they move to a different location they may be in total shadow while the background beyond is bathed in sunshine. In either case the use of fill-in flash will eliminate the shadows or balance the foreground with the background, creating a better shot.

To do this take an exposure meter reading of the highlight area of the picture. Let us imagine it is $1/125$ second

at f11. Set the camera to this exposure. If you are using an automatic flash gun set the aperture dial on it to f 5.6, in other words two stops less than the highlight exposure. If you are using a manual flash gun you will have to work out a combination of aperture and speed from the guide numbers of your flash gun to give you the appropriate exposure. The guide number tells you how strong a flash gun's power is and will alter depending on the speed of the film you are using. For example a film rated at 200 ISO will give a higher guide number than a film rated at 64 ISO.

From the flash gun manufacturer's instructions you can work out the correct aperture to use. Roughly speaking, this is calculated by dividing the guide number by the flash-to-subject distance. Having done this you are now ready to take your shot. The

important point to remember is always to underexpose the flash. If you do not do this then the light from the flash will look too harsh and burn out all the shadow detail. Many photographers are nervous of using fill-in flash because they cannot see the effect it is having until the film is processed, unless of course they have the benefit of Polaroid.

With a reflector, on the other hand, you can see the effect immediately. You can buy custom-made reflectors in a variety of sizes and effects. These range from white and silver through to bronze and gold. Of course you might find yourself in a situation where you do not have a reflector and therefore will have to improvise. A piece of white card, a white sheet or a piece of aluminium foil will do. Let us imagine that the sun is behind your subject. If you hold the reflector so that the sun shines directly onto it you can bounce this light back

● FAR LEFT This picture was taken without the addition of flash.

● LEFT Here the aperture setting on the automatic flash gun was deliberately set at a wider opening than what was required for the available light. This resulted in a weak burst of flash that was just enough to eliminate the shadows under this young woman's eyes. If the same power had been used as for the available light then her face would have been burnt out and the final picture would have looked most unflattering.

to your subject. By changing your position and the angle of the reflector you can redirect the light to exactly where you need it. A silver reflector will give a harsher light than a white one, and a gold one will give a very warm effect. Many photographers prefer using a reflector to fill-in flash as they feel it gives a more natural light.

The use of a reflector or fill-in flash is not just restricted to photographing people. Perhaps you are going to photograph a table outdoors laid for lunch. The table is in the shade but, if you expose for it, then the house in the background, for example, will be overexposed. By using the flash to illuminate the table the two different exposures can be bought into line with one another. Whichever method you decide to use it is of course best to practise before you take some important photographs.

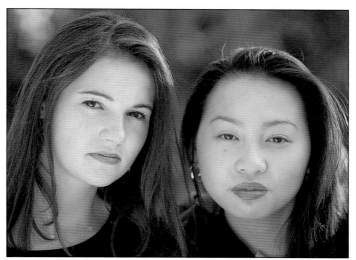

● LEFT These pictures illustrate the difference a reflector makes. In the top picture a white reflector has been used. Although this has bounced the required amount of light back into the subjects' faces it is rather cool. In the second picture a gold reflector makes the quality of the light warmer, giving a more pleasing effect.

● BELOW LEFT In this picture it was important to retain the detail of the house in the background. The exposure for this has meant that some of the items on the table and the owner of the vineyard are in shadow. By using fill-in flash, BELOW RIGHT, these shadows have been softened while still retaining detail. The result is a more pleasing balance between foreground and background.

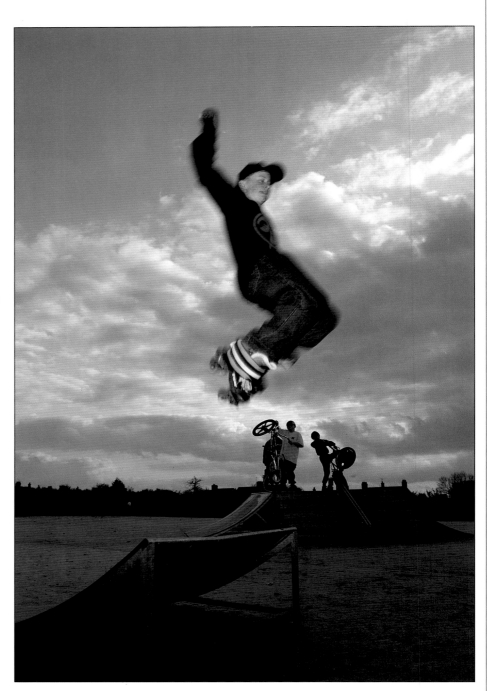

SLOW SYNC FLASH

Flash used normally will freeze a moving object, and, if the exposure is correct, will evenly illuminate everything within its range. But, as in every aspect of photography, creative rule-breaking can produce stunning results; and this is particularly true of the unorthodox technique of slow sync flash.

Most 35 mm SLR cameras have a mark on the shutter speed dial that synchronizes the flash when the picture is taken. Usually this speed is 1/60 or 1/125 second. If a shutter speed faster than this is used the blinds of the focal plane shutter will not have time to open fully, so that part of the picture comes out unexposed. However, it is possible to use a lower speed such as 1/15 or 1/18 second and still synchronize the flash. The flash will not last any longer than usual, which means that it will be illuminating the scene for only part of the time the shutter is open.

If a slow shutter speed is used with flash to photograph a moving object when there is a reasonable amount of ambient light, the subject will be marked by a faint trail looking like 'speed lines' in cartoons. This can look very effective in an action shot such as the picture of a roller skater here.

The important thing is to use a shutter speed compatible with both the ambient light and the desired flash effect. For example, the film is 100 ISO; a meter reading of the ambient light says 1/125 at f5.6. To get the slow sync effect a shutter speed of 1/15 second is needed. To compensate for the difference the aperture should be reduced to f16. Set the dial on the flashgun to f16 or, if it is a manually controlled one, work out the flash-to-subject distance that normally requires an aperture of f16. The result should be worth the effort.

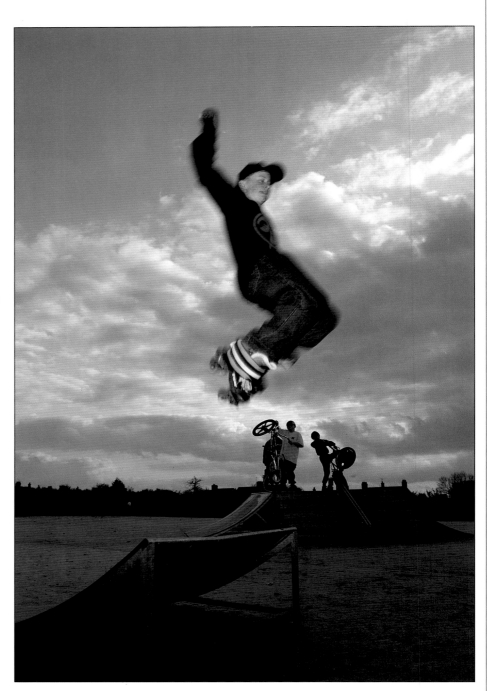

● ABOVE The young boy is almost frozen in mid-flight, even though the shutter speed used was only 1/15 second. This is because he was lit mostly by the flash, not by ambient light. However, the daylight has had a curious effect on his outline so that it looks as if the sky were directly behind him. The ambient light needed a full stop more, but it was decided to underexpose for this to give the shot more impact. The boy's friends in the background complete the composition perfectly.

● RIGHT A similar technique was used indoors to photograph the baby. Here a shutter speed of 1/8 second was used. The baby turned his head as the shot was taken and the flash fired. There was enough ambient light to let this movement show up. It has created an attractive background which increases the effectiveness of the portrait.

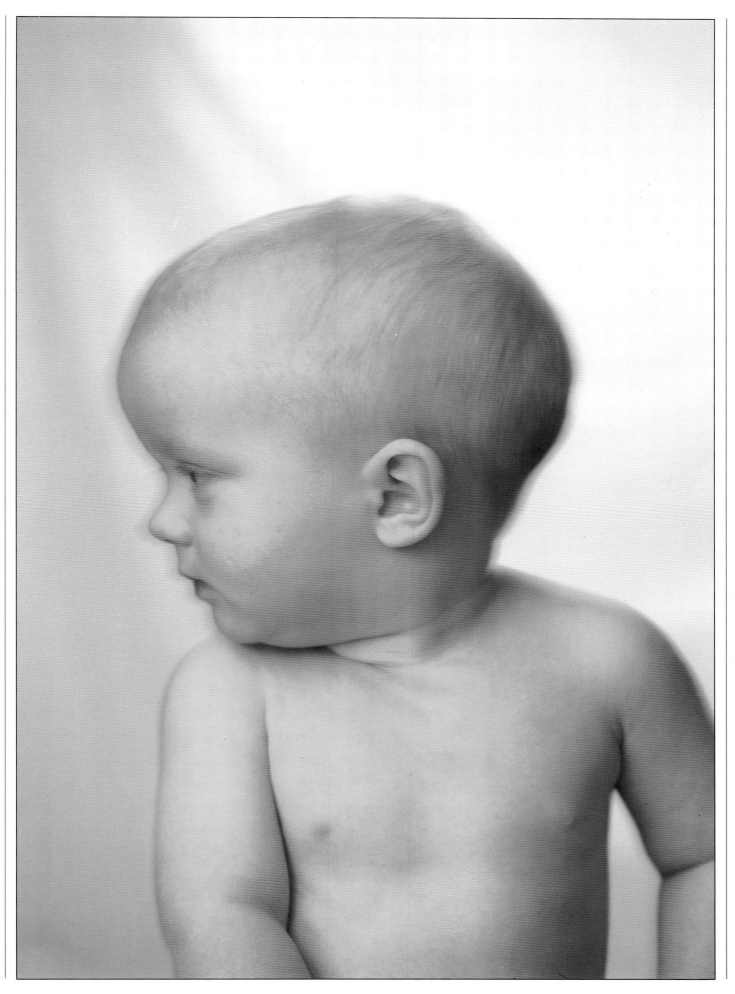

MULTIPLE EXPOSURES

EQUIPMENT & TECHNIQUES

A camera with a facility for multiple exposures – that is, taking more than one picture on the same piece of film – allows unusual images and in the right hands can give stunning effects.

When planning a multiple image shot it is important to remember that light subjects will show up on dark areas. Try to frame the subjects so that a dark area is placed where a subsequent image will have a light subject, or vice versa. Images with large amounts of light areas are not suitable for multiple exposures. For instance, a great area of sky in one image will more or less obliterate anything else that appears in that part of the picture. As with any new technique, practice is necessary.

● BELOW At first glance this picture of the Palace of Holyroodhouse in Scotland may not look like a multiple image. But look at the sky. It is in fact a sequence of ten separate exposures taken at 30 second intervals. Each time the clouds were in a different position. By the final exposure they had moved a considerable way, giving the effect of a celestial explosion.

HOW TO USE VIEWFINDER SCREENS

A range of screens is available for many SLR cameras. A grid screen is best for multiple image shots. It is marked with a grid of vertical and horizontal lines which allows exact positioning of each image. The screen fits under the pentaprism on top of the camera. Release this, take out the existing screen, drop in the new one and put back the prism.

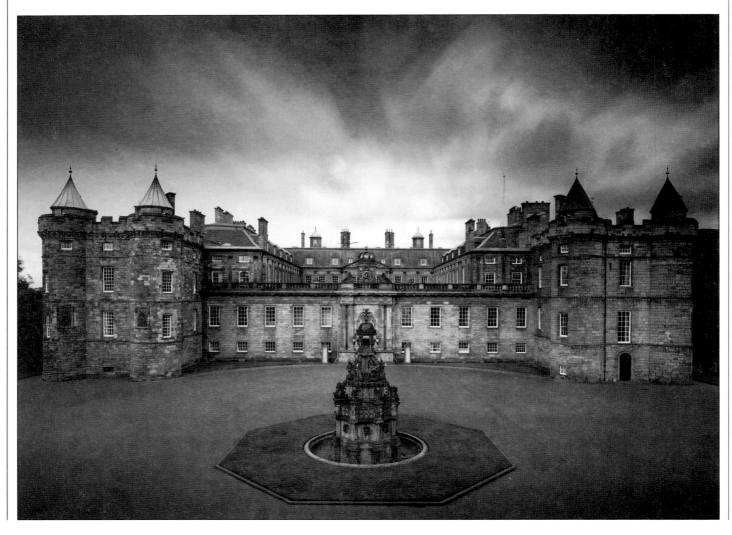

MULTIPLE EXPOSURES WITHOUT SPECIAL FACILITIES

This can be done on many ordinary SLR cameras. It needs some practice to get it right. To take three pictures on one frame, take the first picture in the normal way. Turn the film rewind crank as though rewinding the film back into the cassette, but *do not* press the rewind button. When the slack in the film has been taken up, then press the rewind button. Turn the rewind crank 1½ turns and release the rewind button. Take the next picture and repeat the process. Next take the third picture and then advance the film in the normal way.

● RIGHT This multiple exposure shot was taken indoors against a black background and lit by flash. First, the model was positioned at the left side of the frame, looking to the right. Then he was positioned looking the other way, and the camera was moved so that he was at the right of the frame. The result is a striking shot of both sides of his face in a single image.

● RIGHT The same technique was used in this picture, except that the first image was taken much closer in than the next two. This has made the central image much more dominant than the others. With such a technique care must be taken that the close-up image does not come out distorted.

● LEFT In this sequence of four exposures the camera was moved slightly sideways after each exposure. It is important to avoid making multiple exposure shots simply confusing.

SHOOTING AGAINST THE LIGHT

Many people think that you can only take good photographs if the sun is directly behind or to one side of the camera. Admittedly, by taking shots straight into the sun, flare and incorrect exposure may result, but if handled carefully these can be avoided or used to dramatic effect. To eliminate flare, a good lens hood should suffice. In fact you should always have a lens hood attached to your camera whichever way you are shooting. Flare can result from light indirectly reflecting off a shiny surface such as a car or window as well as directly from the sun.

Calculating exposure needs careful consideration as, if your subject is strongly backlit, it could appear as a silhouette. Although this may be the

effect you are after, an adjustment to exposure will be necessary if you want your subject to be visible. If you are using a camera with built-in metering that has a choice of exposure modes such as average, centre-weighted or spot metering, then the spot metering mode will give a more accurate reading. If your camera only has metering in the average exposure mode, the chances are that it will underexpose your subject.

It is possible to overcome this if you can move in close so that the viewfinder is covering only the subject and take your meter reading at this distance. This means depressing the shutter release button about half-way. If your camera has an autoexposure lock you now keep the shutter release button

● BELOW In this picture the sun is at about 45 degrees behind the young girl. A reflector was used to bounce back a small amount of light into her face. Without this she would have been almost silhouetted against the background. Although a lens hood was used, flare can still be seen in the top left-hand corner of the picture.

● ABOVE By exposing for the light reflecting off the water behind this boy fishing, he is shown almost in silhouette. In this case it works well because it is still obvious what activity he is involved in and the quality of the sparkling light bouncing off the water adds a romantic feel.

● LEFT A combination of a long lens and small aperture have resulted in isolating this plant from its surroundings. The back light has helped to emphasize this effect and the eye is drawn immediately to its delicate blooms.

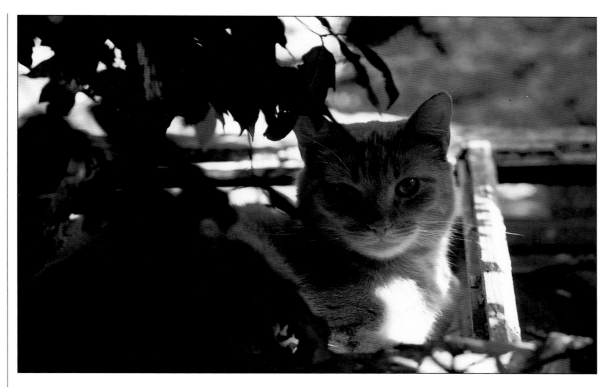

● LEFT Often there is no time to use fill-in flash or a reflector to throw light back onto a subject, and this is often the case with animals. By exposing for the shadows enough detail has been retained to record this cat's peaceful posture in the shade.

slightly depressed and return to your original viewpoint. Without taking your finger off the button take your shot. Your subject will now be correctly exposed although the background will be overexposed. If you are taking more than one shot from this viewpoint you will have to repeat the procedure with each shot.

Another way round this problem is to use the exposure compensation dial – if applicable – on your camera. Set the dial to give two stops more exposure than the reading on the camera meter. If you can operate your camera manually and you have a separate exposure meter then, as above, you could move in close to your subject to take a reading.

If you do use this method with your camera or a hand-held meter, care must be taken not to cast a shadow on your subject, otherwise an incorrect reading will be obtained and overexposure will result. The preferred method of taking a reading with a hand-held meter is to use the incident light method. This means attaching an invercone – a white disc – to the exposure meter sensor. The meter is then pointed to the camera and a reading taken. This method records the amount of light falling on your subject as opposed to reflecting from it.

One word of warning when taking photographs into the light: the sun is very powerful and can be greatly magnified by camera lenses, so if these are pointed to the sun damage to your eyes could result – be careful!

● BELOW By shooting straight into the sun a very dramatic backlit picture has been obtained. A lens hood is essential in a case like this to eliminate flare. Be careful when shooting into the sun that you do not point the camera directly towards it, to avoid damage to your eye.

EQUIPMENT & TECHNIQUES

One of the newest innovations in photography is the video still camera. Unlike conventional cameras, the video still records an image on a small floppy disk, exactly like those used in personal computers. Each disk has the capacity to record up to 50 separate photographs. Instead of sending the disk away to be processed, as would be the case with 35 mm film, the images can be played back instantly on a television screen or computer monitor. They can also be recorded on video tape or run out as prints at the majority of photocopying stores, yet the pictures may not be as good as conventional images.

The video still camera itself looks and is operated in much the same way as a compact camera. It comes with a standard lens but has wide angle and telephoto attachments. It has built-in flash and a tripod adaptor. The exposure selection is automatic and the focus is fixed, but there is a macro facility. Single, multi and self-timer shooting modes, back light control and a rechargeable battery are all standard; it is also a very quiet camera to operate. The conventional rechargeable battery is powerful enough to take 50 shots. An additional power pack is available that will enable you to take 4000 shots. The camera can also be worked directly from the mains as a true 'electronic' camera. There is a time lapse facility which allows a picture to be taken at various intervals, for instance either every minute or up to once every hour.

By using a video controller, the shots can be displayed and previewed backwards and forwards. The viewing sequence can be altered to meet different requirements and recorded on video tape for a permanent display.

● BELOW This picture was originally taken on 35 mm transparency film and then copied onto disk. The print was made using a thermal printer.

● BELOW LEFT By looking at the recorded image on a computer screen, selected parts of a picture can be printed in much the same way as a conventional enlargement. This is a detail of a much larger photograph.

ADVANTAGES OF THE VIDEO STILL CAMERA

- Disks can be stored, edited or used repeatedly.

- The image is stored electronically so there is no need for lengthy conventional processing.

- Unlike conventional film, the disk cannot be 'fogged' and can be exposed to light without incurring any damage.

- Images recorded on disk are instantly ready for viewing just as on video tape.

- A range of accessories, including lenses, are readily available.

● ABOVE This strong image originated from a picture taken on a video still camera of a reflection in a shop window. The camera is at its best when shooting close in, but the scope for abstraction when put into the computer is where your creativity can excel.

● LEFT This full-length portrait was shot using available light filtering through an open window; it was recorded on a floppy disk and printed on a computer thermal printer.

● BELOW Colours can be altered or black and white prints made using a video still camera. This almost monochromatic picture was achieved by manipulating the original disk image in a computer. The scope for different variations and experiments from a single image is endless.

Many compact cameras now have an autofocus facility built in; this allows for even more spontaneity in instant shots. The autofocus camera emits an invisible infrared beam which bounces back off the subject to the camera in much the same way that radar works. The camera analyses this information and sets the focus to the correct distance by means of a small electric motor.

It sounds simple and it is, but there are a few points to remember before shooting the picture. On the most simple autofocus cameras the area analysed by the autofocus mechanism will be in the centre of the frame; it will be this part that the camera focuses on even if the main subject is to one side and therefore out of the autofocus range. It is very simple to learn how to alter the focus by manually overriding this mechanism.

Some of the more sophisticated cameras have a larger area of focus than that of the central spot found in the more simple models. These more sophisticated cameras send out three separate beams and make a 'judgement', either from one of these or from a combination. Many of the single lens reflex cameras that take interchangeable lenses are now of the autofocusing type. Most of these have a manual override for focusing but when in the autofocus mode the same alterations may be required.

1 Shutter release button
– this may also include a pre-set focus control to allow overriding of the autofocus mechanism

4 Autofocus windows
– these send out an infrared beam to judge the focusing requirements of a picture

6 Self-timer indicator lamp
– a blinking light that speeds up as the shutter is about to be released

2 Multifunction LCD and mode controls
– a display panel and controls to measure and adjust additional flash requirements and the self-timer

3 Flash
– this charges up almost instantly and may include a blinking anti-red-eye device

5 Auto exposure metering window
– a light measuring device which judges the amount of light and any flash requirements; some models have a 'spot' reading mechanism

7 Viewfinder
– this gives an accurate visual image of the photograph about to be taken

8 Lens
– this can contain both an autofocus and a zoom facility, allowing for variety in depth of the image

● In this shot the person is in the centre of the frame and is perfectly sharp. The background is out of focus as the automatic focusing mechanism has 'fixed' onto the subject in the foreground. Perhaps the subject needs to be moved to one side in order to reveal or conceal part of the background.

● By repositioning the camera so that the person is at one side of the picture the background comes into sharp focus but the girl is now blurred.

● To eliminate the problem is quite simple. First point the camera at the person and gently depress the shutter release button to a half-way position. This will fix the autofocus mechanism on the subject in the foreground. Keeping the shutter release button depressed, move the camera to the desired position so that the picture is composed satisfactorily. Now depress the shutter release button fully. The picture has now been taken and the person is in focus.

● BELOW Autofocus is excellent for capturing instant and spontaneous shots that retain the essence of a particular moment.

ADVANTAGES OF AUTOMATIC CAMERAS

● Automatic focusing allows spontaneous pictures to be captured instantly without time-consuming dial adjustments.

● The built-in flash provides quick, on-the-spot lighting for every occasion.

● Light exposure is metered automatically, saving on adjustment and measuring time.

● 'Hands-free' pictures can be taken using the self-timer; even the photographer can appear in the shot.

● The small, compact shape makes the camera easily portable in all situations.

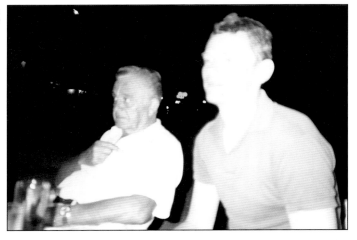

WHEN THINGS GO WRONG

Even when you think you have taken every possible care with your photography, things can still go disappointingly wrong. Often these errors are caused by a momentary lapse of concentration, but in extreme cases the fault can be traced to a malfunction in the camera or other equipment.

Do not be discouraged by faults in your photography; problems are nearly always easy to rectify. Look at the examples shown here and compare your own pictures to diagnose and correct the fault.

Probably the most common fault is fogging of the film. This occurs when the camera back is opened before the film has been fully rewound into the cassette, or because light is leaking into the camera. If light is leaking in, take the camera to a reputable repairer.

If the film is blank when it comes back from the processors, the most likely fault is that the film has not been advancing. When you load the camera, always check to make sure the rewind crank turns when you advance the film; if it does not turn, the film will stay in the cassette.

Consistent overexposure of film may be caused by a defective meter. However, it may also occur if the wrong speed is set or the metering system is set to the wrong ISO speed. Alternatively, this may take place if the aperture on the lens is not stopping down when the shot is taken; this means that the lens needs repairing.

Blurred shots are usually caused by camera shake. This will occur if you are using a slow shutter speed without securing the camera to a tripod. If the camera has aperture priority mode and you are shooting in dull light, the camera will select a slow shutter speed if you choose a small aperture.

● Flash overexposure. Cause: the sensor that determines the power of the flash was covered by part of a hand. To correct: always leave the sensor clear.

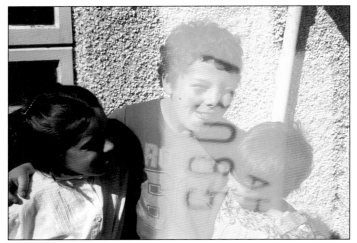

● Flare and marks on the film. Cause: after loading, the film has not been wound on two or three frames before shooting begins. The laboratory's processing marks and number are visible over the image. To correct: always be sure to wind on the film for at least a couple of frames before beginning photography.

● Incorrect framing. Cause: parallax error. When shooting with a compact camera the viewfinder does not see exactly what the lens sees. To correct: refer to the manufacturer's parallax adjustment guide.

● Out of focus. Cause: going too close or incorrect use of an autofocus mechanism so that the middle distance is measured, in this case the plants behind the subject. To correct: semi-depress the shutter on the main foreground subject before framing the shot.

● ABOVE Under-exposure. Cause: the auto-exposure meter has read the reading from the sky rather than from the person. To correct: be sure to take a reading from the main subject.

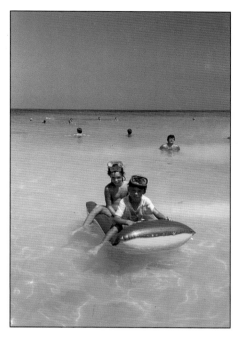

● ABOVE Marks on prints. Cause: the camera back was opened before the film was wound back into the cassette. To correct: ensure the cassette is fully rewound before opening the camera back.

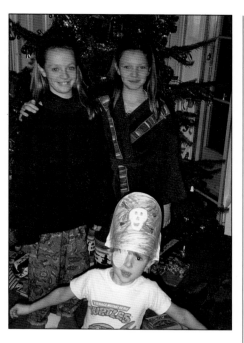

● ABOVE 'Red eye'. Cause: the flash is too close to the lens. To correct: move the flash to one side if possible, or activate the anti-red-eye flash mechanism if one is fitted.

● ABOVE Over-exposed background. Cause: the auto-exposure meter in the camera has taken a reading for the trees in the foreground and over-exposed for the background. To correct: ensure the readings are taken from the main area of interest.

● ABOVE Murky print. Cause: the camera case or a hand is obscuring part of the lens. To correct: ensure the lens is never obstructed.

● LEFT Under-exposure. Cause: the flash is not powerful enough to light the subject properly, as it is too far away, the batteries are weak or a finger is obscuring the flash. To correct: make sure the flash is not obscured, the batteries are fresh and you are positioned correctly within the flash exposure range.

Taking Great Photographs

LANDSCAPES: GENERAL COMPOSITION

The main subject matter of photographs taken while travelling will probably be landscapes. In landscape photography it is very important to take care with composition to avoid producing dull shots, for example of a lot of sky with only a thin strip of land. A commonplace image can be transformed very simply by paying attention to shadow, colour and detail, all of which are paramount in producing good landscape shots.

● LEFT This grouping of trees is common around the River Po in northern Italy. The planting arrangement is exaggerated by going in close using a wide angle lens so that the long lines between the rows form a focal point for the composition. The evening light helps to create a pleasant atmosphere.

● ABOVE Give some thought to which lens to use when composing a landscape shot: it is one of the most important factors in a successful composition. By using a 200 mm telephoto lens this picture has been framed without any sky. The eye is drawn to the slightly pink terrain of the foreground while the grey rock of the canyon forms the background. The long lens has compressed the shot, further emphasizing the foreground. The trees in the foreground look like tiny bushes and this gives an indication of the scale of the canyon.

● LEFT AND BELOW Although these two shots were taken very close to each other, one is a far better composition than the other. In the upright picture the road and tree balance one another, drawing the eye to the centre. The tree is a bold dominant feature; the way the narrow road converges adds a sense of curiosity – what lies beyond? In the horizontal picture the tree appears to lose its dominance and the expanse of fields on either side diminishes the power of the converging sides of the road. It is clear that the smallest adjustment can make a considerable difference to the overall composition.

VARYING A LANDSCAPE SHOT

- Rotate the camera slightly to one side; this may cut out unwanted scenery or bring in an added point of interest.

- Move the camera from a horizontal to a vertical position; sometimes the smallest of movements which does not even involve moving your feet can have a dramatic effect.

- Try isolating a portion of the landscape against a backdrop from a different part of the image; this can emphasize scale or make a coloured field, for example, stand out from surrounding pastures.

- Notice the position of any trees; a single isolated tree or a group of trees apart from a wood or forest can be used as a device for leading the eye into the scene. Tractor furrows or a meandering stream or river have a similar effect.

- An object in one corner of the picture adds to the composition; be careful that there is enough variety in a sequence of shots — do not always place an object in the same corner or the series begins to look dull.

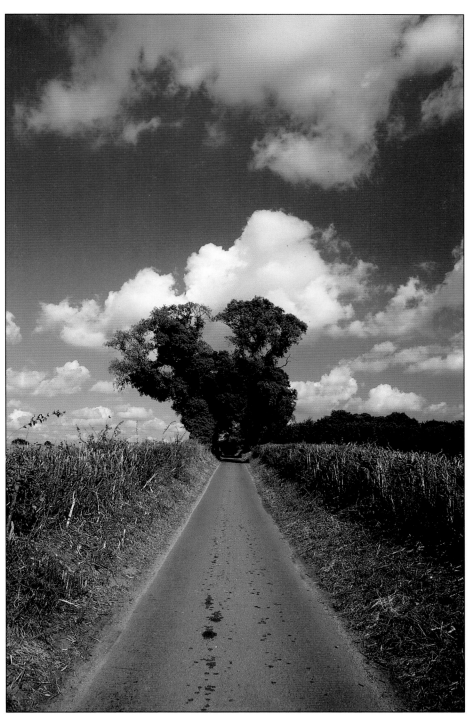

Often the view that looks most spectacular to your eyes does not come out nearly so well on film. This is not necessarily because of any technical fault: it may be just that the wrong viewpoint was chosen when pressing the shutter. All the time you look at anything, your eyes are editing the scene and suppressing uninteresting details. In contrast, the camera records just what is in front of it, and unless you have taken care to exclude things you do not want, they will appear on the print.

In many cases the picture could be improved beyond recognition by moving a short distance. The basic viewpoint may be fine, but perhaps a higher or lower viewpoint is needed; try standing on a step, or crouching down. It is worth taking time to explore a variety of viewpoints. Even when you have taken your shot and are walking away you may suddenly see a better

shot. If you do, take it. After all, film is the least expensive component in photography. You may never return to that place, or the light may never be the same again – so do not worry about using up another couple of frames.

PARALLAX ERROR

One common reason for not getting the picture wanted is parallax error. A camera with a separate viewfinder for the lens – that is, most cameras except single lens reflex cameras – gives a slight difference in framing between what you see and the picture you take. This makes no noticeable difference when photographing a distant object or a landscape, but the closer you go in, the greater the error. If the landscape shot has a foreground you will certainly have to allow for parallax. If you do not, a detail you expect to be in your photograph may simply not appear, and vice versa.

● BELOW, LEFT AND RIGHT From looking at the background of the buildings and cliffs it is clear that both these pictures were taken from almost the same place. But the foregrounds are quite different. This shows the effect that altering the viewpoint slightly can have on the finished picture. Although both compositions work well, the one on the LEFT is taken from a better viewpoint in relation to the sun.

● RIGHT A central viewpoint from a bridge over both the railway track and the canal has created an interesting composition. A fairly slow shutter speed of ¹/₆₀ of a second was used. This has made the express train slightly blurred. But instead of being a fault, it adds an air of movement and speed. In contrast the canal looks calm and tranquil, a bygone and slower mode of transport. The viewpoint contributes greatly to the juxtaposition.

● BELOW Taking this shot from a viewpoint some way up the bank of the lake has brought the pavilion on the far side into clear view. A view from near the water's edge would have made the bridge in the middle distance cut into the pavilion, spoiling the composition.

LANDSCAPES: THE WEATHER

There is no such thing as perfect weather for photography. Of course, photographing people on a beach holiday in the pouring rain may present a few difficulties, but many inclement weather situations are in fact the basis for original and dramatic photographs. Overcast skies can be used to advantage and reveal more about the immediate environment than if the sun were shining on a clear day. Rain can be evocative, portraying isolation and stormy conditions. Wintry, and especially snow-covered views provide good, clear images; these are best shot in sunshine to obtain the best view of the shadows cast on crisp snow – an effect which is lost if the sky is heavy.

Predicting where light will fall is important; try to look at a map to gauge where the sun will shine strongly, and rise and set. Make sure the camera is in position at the right time to get the full effect of the quality of light required, particularly if unusual weather conditions produce dramatic cloud formations.

CAMERA CARE IN EXTREME CONDITIONS

If the weather is very cold the shutter on the camera may freeze and valuable picture opportunities may be lost. Extreme heat can ruin film so keep it wrapped in aluminium foil as this will keep it a little cooler. As big a lens hood as possible may help to shield the lens from the rain; beware of cutting off the corners, or 'vignetting' the picture. Do not let weather conditions prevent photography – be prepared to have a go: the results could be surprising!

● LEFT Mist and fog should not be a deterrent to photographers. This almost monochromatic picture has a strange eerie quality to it. Is the boat perhaps drifting and abandoned? Hazy air can add an enigmatic quality to shots.

● ABOVE AND RIGHT Snow creates wonderful picture possibilities. Take care not to underexpose: there is so much reflected light that exposure meters may read the conditions as being much brighter than they are. Try waiting for different light on snowscenes. Here the picture with the sun shining brightly, RIGHT, certainly enhances the overall effect.

● ABOVE Even in the rain dramatic pictures can be taken. This storm over the Atlantic illustrates the qualities of cold and isolation. A slow shutter speed can help to emphasize the driving rain.

● LEFT Prior calculation of where the sun is going to set means that full advantage can be taken of warm evening light, as here where the sun falls on the shapes of the clouds. The same shot taken earlier in the day would have lacked such intensity, warmth and atmosphere.

● LEFT The heavy rain cloud hanging over the limestone pavement illustrates perfectly the visual effect overcast weather can produce. Here it is particularly apt as the cloud hangs over rock which has been eroded by rainfall over the centuries, so the image has a double purpose, it is visually pleasing as well as instructive.

LANDSCAPES: TIME OF DAY

Throughout the day the sun constantly changes position. In photographic terms this movement is more than one from east to west: any change in the sun will produce a different effect on any landscape. In the early morning and evening the sun will be quite low; the shadows it casts will be long and dramatic. In winter the sun will be lower still and these shadows will be even more exaggerated. At midday the sun will be high and the shadows cast will be shorter. In some cases this can lead to flat and featureless shots, so care must be taken at this time of day.

The other factor to consider is that the light cast by the sun in the early morning and late afternoon will have a warmer tone than that of midday light, so pictures taken at these times will appear redder or more orange than those taken in the middle of the day. It is well worth making the effort to get up early, before the sun rises, to be in position to capture the quality of light as dawn breaks. A little research beforehand will show where the sun will be and what it will fall on, depending on the time of year. Early and late rays of sunlight can illuminate an isolated area of a landscape in much the same way as a giant spotlight trained on the scene.

● ABOVE LEFT This shot was taken at mid-morning, yet there is enough of an angle in the light from the sun to create shadow detail. The well-defined clouds have broken up what could have been a bland sky so that the general result has equal focus and visual impact in all areas.

● ABOVE RIGHT The early evening sun was very low on the horizon when this picture was taken. It has just started to tinge the clouds with red and darken the golden sand. By using a wide aperture, a fast enough shutter speed could be used to capture the gently breaking waves.

● RIGHT AND BELOW RIGHT These two pictures were taken from the same viewpoint, the one BELOW after the sun had set. The sky is bathed in a dramatic red-orange light. In contrast the shot taken in the morning, on the RIGHT, had the sun behind the camera and the quality of light is much cooler. A polarizing filter was used to enhance the colour of the sea.

● LEFT This picture was taken just after the sun has risen and the quality of light is very warm, casting a golden reflection on the River Thames. The early morning mist has diffused the sun and gently bathed the scene with a sense of calm. A little prior research meant that the picture was taken at exactly the time the sun appeared between the dome of St Paul's Cathedral and the National Westminster Bank Tower. If the shot had been taken two months earlier, the sun would have appeared to the right of the tower; four months later it would have been to the left of the cathedral dome.

SEASCAPES

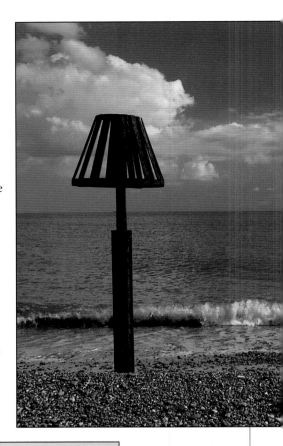

Special care must be taken when photographing seascapes as misleading exposure meter readings can occur. In an environment with so many reflective surfaces the meter can be fooled into measuring the scene as brighter than it is. This can lead to underexposure and disappointing results. To overcome this problem take a meter reading close up of some mid-tone detail.

If the camera is one with built-in autoexposure but no manual override, first decide on the composition. Then point the camera to an area of mid-tone detail such as grey rock. Depress the shutter release button half-way; this will activate the meter and the camera will record the reading. Keeping the shutter depressed in this position, move the camera back to the scene of the original composition. Now gently depress the shutter release button fully and take the picture. To take a similar picture from a slightly different viewpoint, you will have to repeat the process for each shot.

Some cameras with a built-in autoexposure meter have a special mark on the shutter ring labelled AEL, or autoexposure lock, for taking readings like this. Its action is similar to semi-depressing the shutter release button.

● LEFT Movement in the sea at the Giants' Causeway in Northern Ireland is captured and emphasized by a slow shutter speed, to make it look as if the sea is really pounding at the unusual hexagonal rocks that are a famous landmark in this area. The rocks are lit by warm light as sunset approaches, and the strong shadows bring out these strange forms.

● BELOW This picture was taken as a hurricane approached; in high winds it is important to hold the camera steady, perhaps bracing it on a firm surface such as a rock or low wall if you do not have a tripod. Even at relatively fast shutter speeds, such as $1/125$ second, camera shake will lead to blurred pictures.

● ABOVE Always look for points of interest when shooting a seascape. This unusual high tide marker creates a focal point in the foreground while the bright colours of the windsurfer's sail help to create a balance in the overall composition without dominating the scene. Try to imagine the same picture without these two elements. Would it have been as interesting?

● BELOW The addition of a polarizing filter for this shot gives the sea a translucent quality. In order to check the effect of a polarizing filter when using an SLR camera, rotate the filter while looking through the viewfinder, until the desired effect has been achieved.

SPECIAL EQUIPMENT FOR SEASCAPE SHOTS

1 A lens hood – this should be fitted at all times, whether or not beside the sea, but is particularly important in cutting down any unwanted reflections which may flare on the lens.

2 A polarizing filter – this makes the blue colours of the sky much richer and enhances the clarity of any small white clouds. The filter will also change the reflective nature of the surface of the sea.

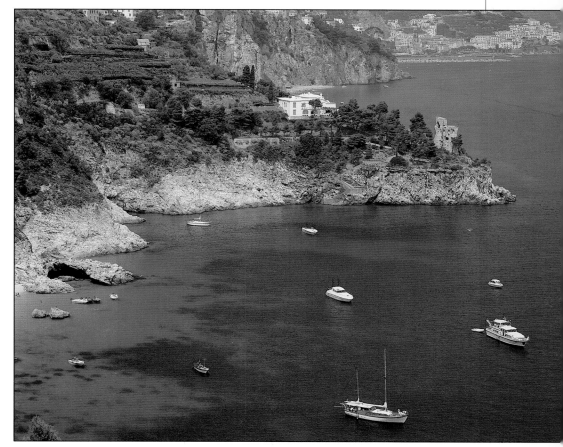

According to the time of year, the ever-changing light, weather conditions, cloud formations and seasonal changes provide an endless range of photographic opportunities when taking pictures of the sky. Although sunsets are a favourite subject for many photographers, not all sky shots need be taken at dusk, and in fact many of the most effective shots are captured at different times of the day.

The essential point to remember when photographing skies is to judge the exposure so that the important details, such as clouds, are recorded. A polarizing filter will help to darken the sky while retaining the detail if the shot is of a blue sky with puffy white clouds. A neutral density graduated filter could be used to similar effect or, for real drama, combined with the polarizing filter. As well as the neutral density graduated filter, a graduated colour filter such as a tobacco graduated filter can be added. This will turn the sky a sepia colour while retaining the natural colour of the land.

When photographing an area you know well, try to be in position early to take advantage of the changing light patterns and the different effects this has on the sky.

When shooting at sunset be prepared to work rapidly as the sun sets very quickly. Also be on the lookout for the changing colour of the sky. Once the sun has set the sky can deepen in colour considerably. At sunset watch for light playing on clouds; an aura of light from these will look far more dramatic than a clear sky. As exposures will be quite long at this time of day a tripod is essential, and a cable release preferable.

● BELOW Here there is an almost perfect mirror image of the sky captured in the surface of the sea. It is best to take this kind of picture when the water is very calm. Watch out for unsightly objects or rubbish floating in the foreground.

● ABOVE This picture was taken just before the sun sank beneath the horizon and its light bathes the few clouds that remain in a golden aura. At this time of day a tripod is essential as the exposure required will be quite long.

REFLECTED SKIES

Skies that reflect into water, for example, make very good subjects. Either try to photograph the water when the air is completely still so that a perfect mirror image is achieved, or isolate a small area of water such as a puddle or pond to create foreground interest.

● LEFT By using a medium neutral density graduated filter all the detail of the clouds has been retained. A wide angle lens combined with a low viewpoint has emphasized the sky and it dominates the picture.

● RIGHT This shot was taken just before sunset. By using the small amount of water in the foreground interest is focused on the sky and the composition greatly enhanced. The backlighting on the ripples of the wet sand has added texture. In a situation like this carefully consider the reflective surface from various positions to obtain the best viewpoint.

*B*UILDINGS

Buildings present the photographer with an inexhaustible supply of imagery. The most important part of photographing any building is the general composition. The weather can be perfect, the exposure correct and the time of day just right, but a badly-framed picture will ruin everything. Here, equipment can be a great help:

● a telephoto lens will not only bring closer a distant building but also, depending on the power of the lens, compress the overall view and so reduce the illusion of space between the main building in the shot and those that may be behind or in front of it.

● a wide angle lens allows a close-up shot with an exaggerated perspective. A tall building such as a skyscraper can appear even taller if the camera is pointed upwards because the verticals will converge.

● a shift lens allows the photographer to avoid converging verticals in situations where these are not wanted as part of the shot. A shift lens alters the axis of view without the need to move the camera, yet allows movement of the lens in relationship to the film plane.

Choosing the correct viewpoint is a vital ingredient for general composition. Position the camera so that there are no unwanted objects within the frame. This may mean simply moving a short distance or using a different lens. If the camera is fitted with a zoom lens all that may be needed is a small adjustment in its focal length.

● ABOVE A telephoto lens was used for this shot of an isolated Scottish house; the top of the mountains that form the backdrop was deliberately cropped out. By composing a picture in this way the isolation of the subject is emphasized and becomes a particular point of focal interest.

● LEFT A small telephoto lens of 100 mm was used for this shot. This slightly compresses the buildings making the composition very tight. Ensure that any vehicles or other unwanted intrusions have been moved before taking the shot, or try to stand in a position where they would be cropped out of the frame.

● ABOVE The railings around the church form a frame for this picture and produce a pleasing composition. Although a wide angle lens was used the viewpoint was close enough to prevent the church receding too far into the distance. The puffy white clouds help to break up the blue sky and enhance the composition, adding another visual element.

● ABOVE By waiting until dusk a certain quality of light is captured; here the tower is bathed in a warm glow. The reflection of the building in the water helps to give a greater illusion of height. The use of a shift lens means that there are no converging verticals, yet the whole building still fits the frame. Remember to ensure that when photographing modern buildings light is not reflected off their exterior surfaces and into the camera lens.

FLORA

Plants provide good material for the photographer. It is worth considering not only exotic plants but also more commonplace varieties. Apart from colour, texture plays an important part in a striking image. All plants look their best at a certain time of year. If any plant is of particular interest, check when it is in season, especially if you have to travel any distance to photograph it.

Original effects can be created by isolating one plant in a mass of others, perhaps using the shallow depth of field afforded by a telephoto lens. There are other opportunities for unusual viewpoints; for instance a plant or group of flowers, or even trees in the foreground of a scene adds interest in its own right and can also mask an unwanted object that would otherwise spoil the picture.

● BELOW By using extension rings it was possible to get very close to this marigold. Depth of field was very limited and a long exposure was needed. This meant that the camera had to be mounted on a tripod and a shield used to protect the plant from wind, so that it did not move and blur the picture.

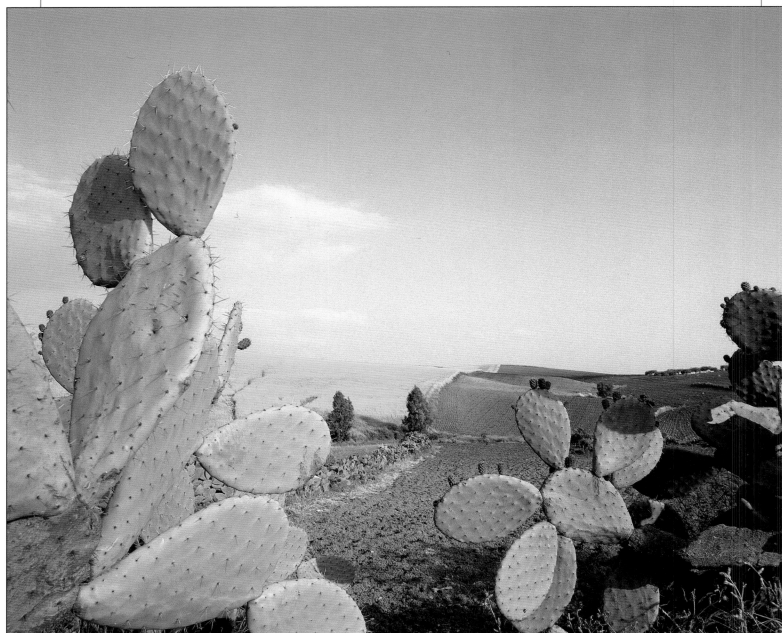

CLOSE-UPS

- If you are taking close-ups of flowers, depth of field will be very small, especially if you are using extension rings or bellows. You will therefore need to stop down as much as possible, and to use a long exposure. If there is even the slightest breeze the plant will have to be sheltered from it, or it will sway and blur the picture.

- Lighting can also be a problem when working so close. If you are using available daylight you must take care not to cast a shadow from yourself or your equipment. A ring flash could be a useful accessory. This gives powerful but almost shadowless illumination. The flash tube forms a complete ring around the lens. Units for 35 mm cameras are quite compact and do not weigh very much.

- A tripod is essential because of the length of exposures.

- Details of trees and other plants are also excellent subjects for close-up shots. The texture of bark can be fascinating, and different shots can be mounted together to make a striking collage.

● ABOVE RIGHT Look for the unusual. There will always be something of interest on a country walk. This whitebell was growing alone in a sea of ordinary bluebells. Careful use of depth of field has put the background out of focus, making the flower even more prominent in the picture.

● RIGHT The texture of tree bark can be very satisfying, especially when several varieties are mounted together. A whole series of pictures can be built up over the years. This applies equally to many other natural forms.

● LEFT These cacti in the foreground frame the view. Not only do plants in the foreground add to the general composition, they can also be used to hide unsightly objects such as telegraph poles.

*F*AUNA

● BELOW Safari parks provide ample opportunity for photographing wildlife. A telephoto lens is essential as animals like this lion can only be photographed from a safe distance. Sometimes autofocus lenses do not work effectively when photographing through glass objects like car windows. Manual focusing can overcome this problem.

One of the most demanding areas of photography is that of wild or semi-wild animals. Patience is required, and a certain amount of forward planning is useful if not essential. Despite the arduous nature of this area, the rewards can certainly make it worthwhile. While most people do not have the opportunity to travel to the regions best suited to photography of big game or endangered species, many may live within reach of a farm or a safari or wildlife park. Safari parks have many exotic animals and with some peaceful species such as the zebra or giraffe it is sometimes possible to leave the vehicle and stand in the same area to take the shot with a medium telephoto lens of 100–200 mm.

● ABOVE If taking a photograph in a safari or wildlife park or zoo, a natural image is perfectly possible as long as the background includes relevant vegetation rather than an unsightly man-made intrusion. A close-up shot can be obtained without frightening the animal by using a 100 mm lens.

● ABOVE Small details are always most effective, especially when photographing fauna. These flamingoes look as if they are asleep yet a careful look at the far bird shows that its eye is open. This shot was taken with a 250 mm lens since if the camera had been positioned any closer the birds would have moved away.

PHOTOGRAPHING WILD ANIMALS

● Spend some time observing the behaviour of the animal; watch to see whether it is easily startled, or whether it appears to move in a constant direction.

● Try to select a viewpoint with an interesting background without unsightly fences or buildings.

● Be patient. Calling or gesturing to an animal will probably cause it to run in the opposite direction. Upsetting wild animals can also be dangerous: however docile they may seem it is important to remember that they are wild. It is best to avoid annoying both the animal and the farmer or ranger.

● BELOW Always be on the look out for spontaneous pictures. A quick check for any unsightly intrusions is usually all that is needed towards the composition of such shots.

● ABOVE This shot of cattle was taken in close from a higher viewpoint. All detail has been cropped out leaving only the black and white hides visible. This technique produces some effective graphic images that usually need a second look before the viewer realizes what the apparently abstract image is.

● RIGHT This shot was taken from a low viewpoint with a wide angle lens. This produces a dramatic image of the sky. By getting into position and being patient it is relatively easy to obtain effective and at times amusing shots of certain animals, whose natural curiosity means that they eventually come close to the camera for a better look. In this shot, the shutter was fired when the cow was about 3 ft (1 m) from the camera.

● BELOW By cropping the picture tightly – a medium telephoto lens was used – any extraneous details can be excluded. The texture of the wall provides a perfect canvas for setting off the doorway, the shrub and the traffic sign.

Travel often has the effect of making us more visually alert. Many things in our day-to-day lives may pass us by without us giving them a second glance. However, a new environment provides visual stimuli; to the photographer these stimuli provide a new awareness of photographic possibilities. Many items around us may not be very interesting in themselves, but gathered together in a collection, perhaps as a grouping of souvenirs from a particular place and photographed in an attractive way, a still life picture is created.

Still life arrangements have inspired painters throughout time and the same inspiration provides photographers with numerous creative opportunities. It is a useful discipline to look closely at, and arrange and light a group of inanimate objects. Sometimes these arrangements already exist and all that is required is to see the potential for an attractive shot.

● LEFT This is a good example of a ready-made still life. All the objects were fixed to the side of a barn on a ranch in Arizona. This shot frames them to their best advantage; no other preparation was needed. To the ranch owners this was just an assortment of objects rather than a creative arrangement. It is often worth looking around at familiar objects to view them with a fresh eye.

● RIGHT Some still life arrangements present themselves; this collection of African craft objects and furniture was lying in the corner of a room, lit by weak sunlight coming through an open window. A white reflector to the right helped throw back just enough light to illuminate the shadow areas.

● BELOW RIGHT A large aperture was used to emphasize the colour of these flowers by minimizing depth of field and throwing the background out of focus. The lines of the steps beyond are still just discernible and lift the background so that it remains a composite part of the picture without being too bland.

CHECKLIST FOR STILL LIFE SHOTS

● Should the arrangement be lit with flash or is there enough available light?

● Examine the available light for any creative elements: does a shaft of light fall at just the right angle?

● Which angle would look best for the shot? Imagine the arrangement in the centre of a circle. Stand a certain distance from the objects and walk around them slowly, stopping at regular intervals. Every pause provides a new visual angle and a different shot.

● Which viewpoint? Consider the arrangement from eye level, as well as from above and from below.

● Every visual angle provides a different background: which one is most suitable and complements the objects most effectively?

● Consider the depth of field: should the background be sharp or blurred?

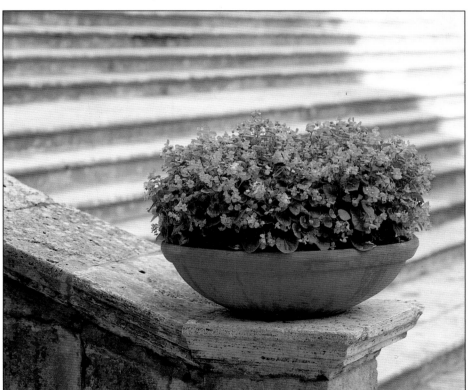

PATTERNS

The refreshingly new viewpoints that travel often provides may reveal scenes or details that appear isolated from their immediate surroundings. This might be due to the way the light falls or may be because of an object's texture, or a combination of both these elements. Such images need not be confined to a documentary record of a place but can be used to startling creative effect. Examine the patterns created by an object or group of objects; often when such objects or scenes are carefully framed they form an interesting composition. Sometimes the pictures have a very abstract appearance or they may need careful viewing to see exactly what they are.

It is important to examine all the possibilities of a scene before taking the shot:

● Would it look best if framed symmetrically?

● Do the lines of perspective increase or decrease with the chosen viewpoint? If so, which is best?

● Is texture an important part of the picture? If so, does the light need to come from the back or the side to emphasize the texture?

● Would going in close help to achieve the effect better than being positioned further back?

● Would using a wide angle or a fisheye lens create a more interesting or subtle effect? This can be especially striking when looking up at the ceiling of a building, for instance, particularly if all the horizontal and vertical lines have been carefully aligned.

● Consider using prints or transparencies in a collage of different patterns. Try reversing one of the pictures and butting it up to one that is the correct way round.

⬡ EVENTS

All over the world events take place which are worth a special journey. One such is London's Notting Hill Carnival, the largest street festival in Europe. People flock from far afield to see the parade, dance and share the street parties. Some come for that reason alone, others as part of a wider tour of the city or the country.

GETTING IT RIGHT

If you decide to make an event the high point of your trip, a little planning will avoid disappointment. Make sure you arrive at the right time: this may sound obvious, but events do not always happen on the same date each year, especially if they are associated with a movable festival such as Easter (which also happens on a later date for the Orthodox Church).

Take plenty of film. This will help to keep your pictures consistent, as they will all be from the same emulsion batch. With film bought locally you can never be sure how long it has been lying around in the shop, perhaps exposed to damaging heat. You often see film being hawked around tourist sites unshielded from the blazing sun.

Professionals keep their film refrigerated. You cannot take a refrigerator with you, but at least you can keep your film as cool as possible.

CHOOSING A THEME

At huge and varied events it is difficult to get just one picture that says everything. That is not to say that you should not look out for such a shot. A better approach might be to shoot as much as you possibly can, and to assemble these pictures as a montage on a particular theme, or a diary of events. Themes could be faces, floats, costumes, food, or the onlookers themselves. Many events last for several days, so you will have plenty of time to get all your shots.

SECURITY

Events such as the Carnival are also a magnet for pickpockets. If you are carrying a case for accessories keep it properly secured at all times. Be alert for children who beg you to take their picture. It sometimes happens that, while you are concentrating on the shot, one of their colleagues is lifting your valuables.

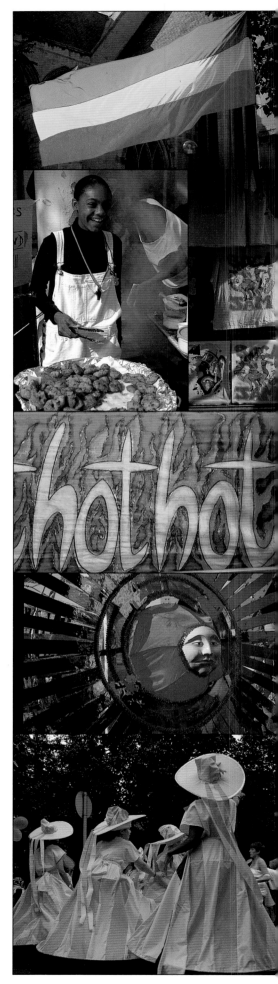

● A collection of images placed together effectively captures the atmosphere of London's Notting Hill Carnival. Small details can be placed next to wider shots of dancers and street scenes to convey the sense of colour and exuberance.

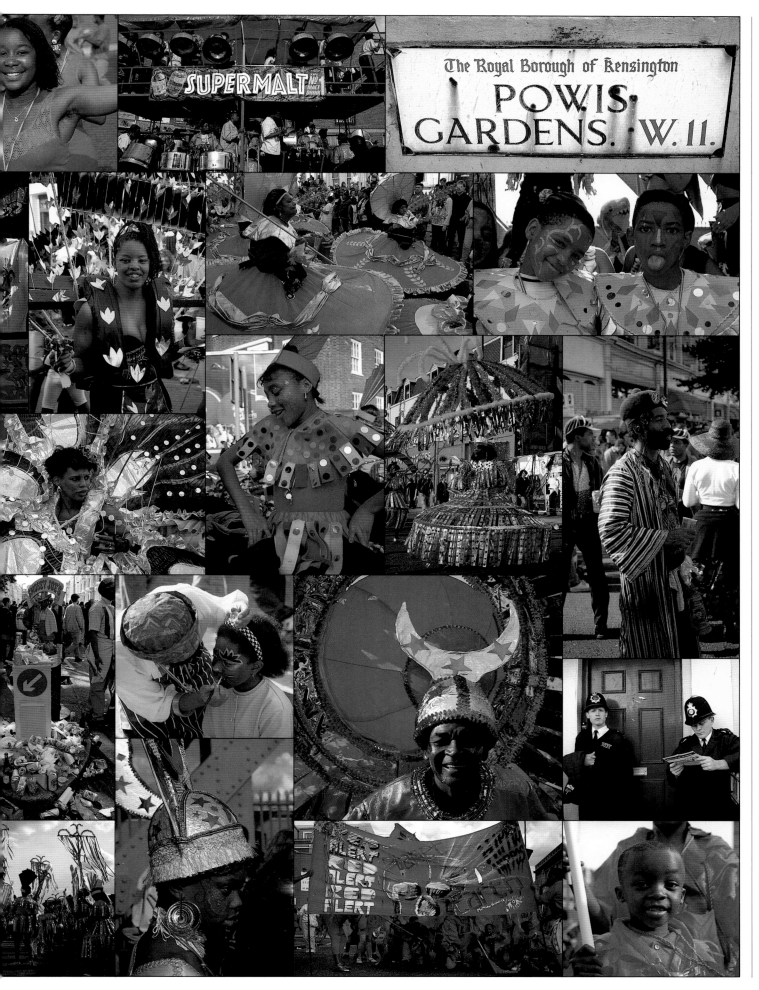

FORMAL PORTRAITS

Formal portraits do not mean that subjects have to sit or stand to attention so that they look stiff and uncomfortable. In the early days of photography when exposure times were measured in minutes people did have to sit very still to avoid blurring the picture. Photographers even used special clamps at the back of their sitter's neck and waist to brace them in position. Fortunately these days are long past.

The most important thing in any portrait, formal or otherwise, is to capture the expression that best illustrates a person's character or status, or both. However formal the portrait might be, try to enter into a dialogue with the sitter. Discover a common interest, and the conversation will become easy and relaxed.

Even if the sitter is a complete stranger, try to plan the general nature of the shot in advance. It makes a bad impression if the first thing the photographer does after meeting the sitter is to stare hard at him, as if undecided what to do. But it is also important to plan wisely; it produces an even worse impression if, after a few shots, it becomes clear that the setting does not work, so that all the equipment has to be altered.

Often, time is of the essence. Some people, such as businessmen and public figures, are very busy, and they may be under the impression that photographs can be taken as quickly as if they had walked into an automatic photo booth. Knowing what is wanted, and directing sitters with flair and firmness, can yield strong portraits in a relatively short time. The results will please them and enhance the photographer's reputation and they are more likely to return.

● ABOVE Although this portrait of a young girl was taken in a studio, it is full of flair and vitality. An immediate rapport was struck up with her so that she felt confident and relaxed. Atmosphere is very important in any situation where there is close communication between photographer and model. It would be disastrous to start a session in an atmosphere of tension; this is as true in the studio as it is on location.

● LEFT This room looks grand and formal, yet the woman's expression gives the portrait warmth and there is the impression that it was a relaxed photographic session. Both the room and the hallway which is visible through the far doorway had to be lit. If the door had been shut the atmosphere might have seemed a little claustrophobic. Being able to see beyond the room adds space and light. Although the picture takes a wide view, there is no doubt that the woman is the centre of attention.

● RIGHT Formality need not mean rigidity. In this portrait of the photographer Terence Donovan the composition's formality and symmetry give him an enigmatic quality. For those who do not know his reputation as a photographer there are a few props to give a clue to his profession. Terence Donovan also runs a very successful film production company, and there is just a hint of the entrepreneur here.

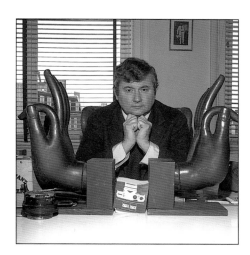

● RIGHT The portrait of the former Speaker of the House of Commons in London had to be taken in a 10-minute session. His gown and wig might have made him look intimidating and rigid; instead they signify the status of his position and are in keeping with a portrait that is both formal and interesting. Although the Speaker appears small this is in effective contrast to the grandeur of the room.

INFORMAL PORTRAITS

Many portraits work because they have an informal look that most people would call 'natural'. But even pictures like these need thought to make them successful. For instance, it is pointless to take lots of pictures in a casual manner if the exposure or focus are incorrect or the shot is badly composed. With a little forethought all these problems can be avoided, but at the same time there is no need to be so preoccupied with the mechanics of photography that it causes inhibition and the pictures become rigid and unspontaneous.

As with all aspects of photography, the most important thing is being so familiar with the equipment that all the controls become second nature. Once these are mastered it is possible to concentrate on technique and become more adventurous.

This might mean experimenting with a different type of film. Try a high-speed one such as 1600 ISO. This will give very grainy results, but that is by no means an unattractive effect, as one of the pictures here shows. Also, using such a fast film allows pictures to be taken in almost any conditions. The film can even be uprated to 3200 ISO. (Remember that if this is done the whole film has to be shot at this rating, and when giving the film to the processing laboratory the technicians must be told that it has been uprated so that they can increase development time.)

A zoom lens, especially when combined with an autofocus mechanism, makes for faster work since focal length can be changed without the need to swap lenses.

Ultimately, of course, it is the photographer's eye that seizes upon that good shot, however much advanced equipment may be available!

● ABOVE This picture radiates spontaneity, warmth and humour. It is a good example of capturing the moment, which swiftly passes when dealing with animals. Going in close helps the general composition and focuses attention on the woman and the chicken.

● BELOW Pictures like these come readily to the alert photographer. Always have the camera loaded with film to avoid wasting time. The person might move away – or in this case merely put on his socks and shoes.

● ABOVE An ultra-fast film, 1600 ISO, has perfectly caught this young boy's cheeky expression. The grainy quality of the film, far from being a drawback, adds to the picture. The day was dull and the area surrounded by trees, so it is unlikely that a slow film would have given an adequate picture. Especially with informal portraits, be ready to try something different and do not be afraid to push film to its limits.

● RIGHT This couple was photographed informally at a barbecue. Using a 100 mm lens makes them fill the frame without the need to go so close as to make them feel uncomfortable. Her vivacious smile contrasts attractively with his rather whimsical expression. The result is a natural look that is relaxed and charming.

● BELOW Even when going in close, it is still possible to achieve a relaxed portrait. The old man's weathered face is set against a plain background which isolates and emphasizes his face. The ladder acts as a prop and introduces an informal element into the composition. The man's open-necked shirt adds a carefree element without looking untidy.

PEOPLE IN THE HOME

● BELOW Children like helping around the house and such occasions can provide good opportunities for pictures, especially if there is a camera loaded and ready. Even better, this should be a simple model that anyone can use. If it is loaded with medium to fast film such as 200 ISO, it should cope with most situations without flash being necessary.

Many people do not take pictures at home except on special occasions such as a birthday or Christmas. But there are many other times when opportunities for photographs present themselves, and often these can lead to excellent portraits. One advantage of taking pictures at home is that people feel relaxed because they are in their normal environment. Another is that they are surrounded by objects that reflect their personality, which can be brought into pictures as props or backgrounds; these will reveal the varied aspects of their way of life, and their interests.

There is plenty of opportunity for spontaneous pictures in the home, especially of children. They may be doing the most ordinary, everyday things but even these, when viewed through the camera, can be seen in a new light, and spontaneous actions captured. This is one reason why it is so important to be ready with your camera. If it seems laborious to get out all your equipment, one solution is to buy an inexpensive compact camera for use around the house. This can always be kept loaded and ready to hand. It should have a built-in flash for quick shots in all conditions. In this way there will never be a reason to miss a picture – and many pictures will be well worth the effort.

● BELOW This informal picture of a young girl at the piano needed flash. The piano keys make an interesting background. The high viewpoint adds to the picture's informality.

● BELOW LEFT This couple photographed in their conservatory is a good example of balancing flash with daylight. The picture looks as if everything is lit by daylight, but in fact if flash had not been added the foreground and the couple's faces would have been in deep shadow. It was a day of patchy cloud with the sun going in and out, so it needed patience to wait for the sun to shine – but the result was worth it.

● BELOW Although this portrait is posed it has a relaxed feel to it. The musical scores in the fore-ground hint that the subject is a composer, or at least that music is important to him. Two flash units were used. One was directed at the man and the foreground, the other to light the area behind. These were balanced so that the scene outside the window was correctly exposed as well.

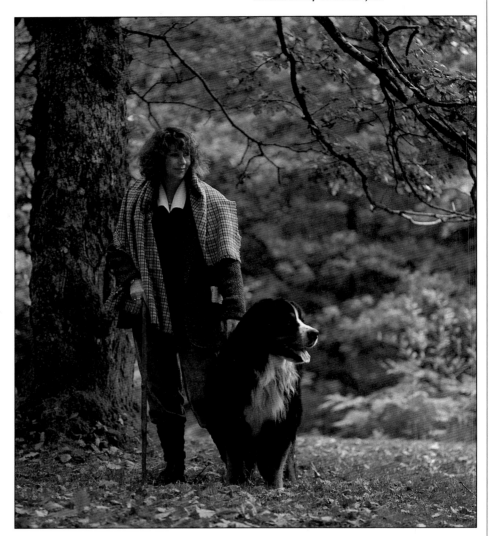

OUTDOOR PORTRAITS

● BELOW Even on a dull overcast day good pictures can be taken. Photographing this person out walking her dog against a wooded background has cut out the dull sky. A 250 mm lens has reduced the depth of field, so that the focus is firmly on the subject.

Bright, sunny days offer good opportunities for taking portraits outdoors. But they can cause problems too. Bright sunlight can create harsh shadows. It can also make people screw up their eyes and squint, which looks most unattractive. To get round this problem, try to move the person being photographed into an area of shade. Alternatively, turn them away from direct sunlight and use a reflector to throw light back into their face. If the person is wearing a hat and the brim is casting a shadow across their face, use fill-in flash to soften the shadow.

Another problem with portraits outdoors is that the wind blows people's hair about and leaves it looking messy. If possible, look for an area sheltered from the wind.

Be on the look-out for appealing backgrounds. This could be something with an interesting texture, such as a stone wall, or it might be a view into a landscape. If the background is not photogenic, consider ways of cutting it out. This can be done by going in close and framing the picture tightly, or by using a large aperture to throw the background out of focus.

When photographing groups of people make sure that one does not cast an ugly shadow on another.

Bright but hazy days give an even, shadowless light, but in certain conditions and with some colour films the results may be a little cool. To alleviate this problem try using an 81A filter. This will slightly warm up the tones.

● RIGHT These young girls form a well-proportioned group. They were photographed with the sun to one side and slightly behind them. This has avoided ugly shadows under their eyes, and stopped any one of them from shading another. The background is dominated by the pool; the wall is unobtrusive and does not spoil the composition.

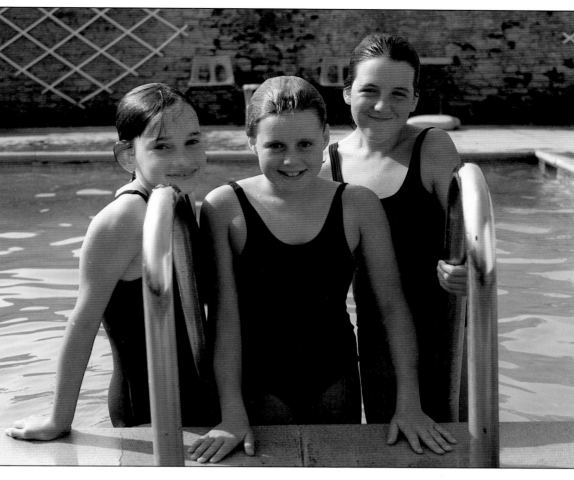

● LEFT Focusing directly on this man's eyes shows the full character of his face. Every detail of his beard is sharp. He was photographed under a white blind that acted as a diffuser so that the light, although bright, does not cast any shadows on his face.

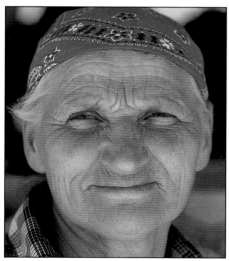

● ABOVE In this picture of an elderly woman, a 100 mm medium telephoto lens combined with a wide aperture has put the background out of focus. It has made the splash of green behind the subject unobtrusive, but the colour complements that of her headscarf. She is in a relatively shaded area, so that her face glows with an even, natural light.

● RIGHT A low viewpoint and going in quite close lets this boy dominate the picture. The surrounding landscape gives a feeling of spring, and the boy's expression is one of playfulness. When taking portraits out of doors experiment with different viewpoints. Otherwise pictures will have an air of sameness.

Poor weather does not have to deter you from photographing people. Sometimes it can actually add to and animate a photograph. But before taking your camera out in pouring rain, remember that cameras should not get wet. A camera that gets thoroughly soaked — or worse still, dropped in the sea — will probably be irreparably damaged.

If the skies are full of fast-moving clouds with quick bursts of inter-mittent sunshine, extra care will have to be taken with exposure. If the sun is out when you take your reading but behind cloud when you take your shot, the photograph will be underexposed. The reverse will be true if the sun is obscured when you take your reading but then comes out before you take your shot.

Look out for something unusual that will lift your shots in poor weather, and give them a point of interest. An isolated colour, or a solitary figure in a landscape, will dispel the grey look. Whatever happens, do not be deterred by poor weather conditions.

● LEFT Here is a good example of making the best of a picture in poor weather, as people cross Dublin's Halfpenny Bridge in the pouring rain, their umbrellas jostling for space. The two large coloured umbrellas stand out in an otherwise monochromatic scene. The picture was taken inside a doorway which helped protect the camera from the rain.

● ABOVE As you go for a walk on a dull, overcast day, you are all the more likely to notice a splash of colour that can make all the difference to a photograph. The flag on the beach marked the area of safe bathing. It was pure coincidence that the red and yellow of the flag matched the colours of the children's oilskins. Even something as simple as a patch of colour can enliven the dullest of scenes. Be prepared at all times for the chance of a spontaneous shot.

KEEPING YOUR CAMERA DRY

- If you are with other people, have them hold an umbrella over you. If not, try to stand beneath some shelter.

- A lens hood will protect your lens from rain. If the lens does get splashed, wipe the drops off immediately with a soft cloth or lens tissue. If you do not do this, they will show up on your photographs as unsightly out-of-focus blobs.

- A plastic bag put over the camera when you are not using it provides quite good protection from the wet.

● ABOVE A close-up of a girl in the pouring rain shows just how animated a poor-weather shot can be. Her brilliant smile and bright eyes express fun and cheerfulness, even though she is getting soaked. Going in close puts the emphasis on her rather than the dreary background. A lens hood protected the lens from splashes.

● RIGHT Although this shot was taken in the summer a dull sea mist was drifting inland from the coast. The isolation of the child looking for shells on the beach is emphasized by the mist. The Victorian railway viaduct in the background helps to relieve the gloom. If there had been more people in this shot they would have distracted from the image of the private world the child inhabits.

HOLIDAYS

More photographs are taken on holiday than at any other time. Obviously there is an incentive to get good shots of family or friends, not to mention new and interesting buildings and scenes.

There are a few points to remember before setting off: take plenty of film; make sure that all equipment is in working order and that any batteries are fresh. For a beach holiday, take a plastic bag to protect the camera from sand as it can ruin lenses. If any gets on the front element, blow it off – cleaning the lens with a cloth would have the same effect as sandpapering it.

Bright sunlight can cast deep and unattractive shadows under people's eyes so it is important to think about portable lighting equipment. Flash can be used to fill in these shadows. Another solution is to use a reflector to throw light back onto the subject's face. At the seaside there are vast areas that reflect light, and it is easy to be misled by the reading given by a light meter. If possible take a meter reading from a neutral area.

Look out for spontaneous shots. Candid shots, even of total strangers, can make a good picture – competitions have been won by such pictures so be prepared for that instant shot.

Wherever the scene of the holiday, it is likely that there will be some event such as a fair or festival. These provide local colour, and should be used to advantage. They can include information about customs and traditions which adds an air of authenticity and situation to the shot.

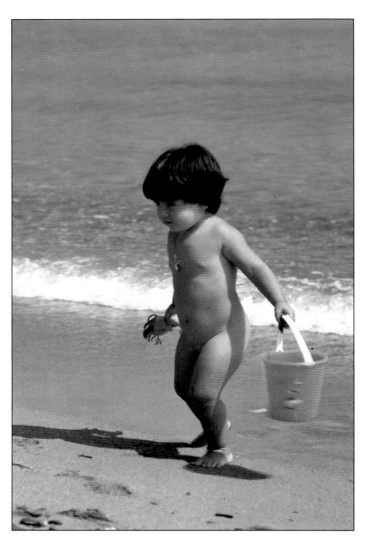

● LEFT Young children make delightful subjects, none more so than this boy with his bucket. Be careful with exposure in seaside shots, since the glare from the sea and beach can fool the meter into underexposing the subject.

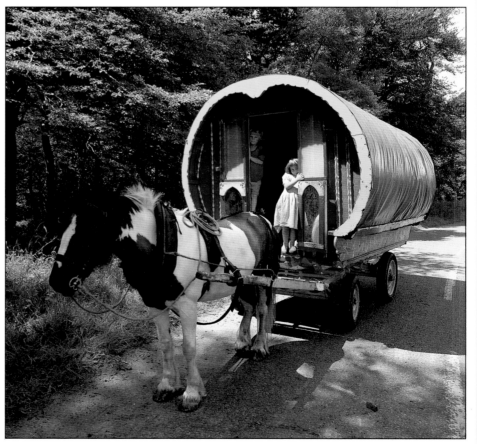

● RIGHT These children were on a Romany caravan holiday in Ireland. They were slightly reluctant to be photographed, but agreed as long as the horse and caravan were included in the shot.

● BELOW Although slightly posed, this picture of a young girl at a swimming pool is an attractive holiday portrait. The line of the white wall adds to the composition and makes an effective contrast with the blue of the pool. Shots like this can be fun, but it is important to work quickly so that being photographed does not become a chore for the child – boredom cannot be disguised.

● BELOW In the holiday season most countries provide good set-piece events. Events can happen spontaneously, so be prepared. It is important to get the best viewpoint for a shot, as far as this can be done without being rude or pushy. Failing this, hold the camera above the heads of the crowd and point it at the action – it may be an outside chance, but it could work!

● ABOVE This picture taken from a high viewpoint shows what can be achieved by looking for a new and striking angle. Seen from above, the water is translucent. The dinghy adds a splash of colour. The two boys did not know they were being photographed, and the spontaneity of this simple shot adds to its effect.

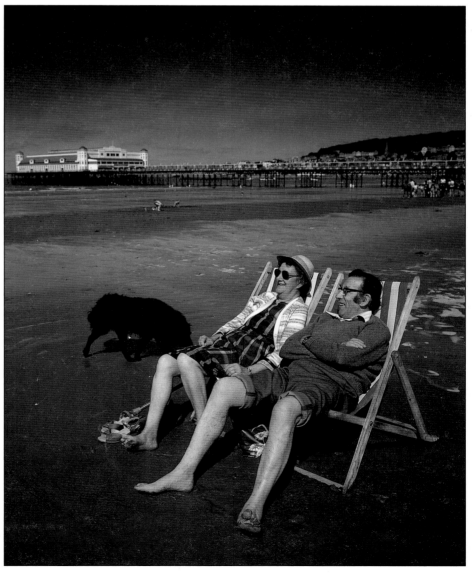

● RIGHT This couple fits in well with most people's idea of the British on holiday. The photographer did not know the people, but they happily agreed to be photographed. The picture is full of good-natured humour. Only a camera ready for instant use will capture the mood in this way.

When photographing children it is often a good idea to include their mother. She is usually the closest person to the child and the best suited to allay its fears and put it at ease, and help it to adopt the best position.

Use a photographer's eye to look for the best viewpoint and lighting to show the natural bond between mother and child. As in any situation when photographing more than one person, be careful that the mother's head does not cast a shadow on the child's face.

If working indoors try to use available light. This will be less distracting to the child, which may be alarmed if flash is used. If flash is necessary, soften the light as much as possible. This can be done by bouncing the light off a suitable surface such as a white ceiling or board. Alternatively

put a diffuser over the light. This can be tracing paper or even a handkerchief. Take care here not to underexpose the photograph. The best way to avoid this is to use a flash meter, which shows exactly how much light is falling on the subject. If the mother and child are sitting by a window, a reflector can be used to throw some natural light back on them.

When working out of doors make sure that neither the mother or child gets cold. Not only is it uncomfortable for them, but they might be shown with red hands and dripping noses.

Above all, be aware that most children can only concentrate for a short time. This may mean working quickly. Conversely, a good deal of patience may be required to catch the child at the best moment.

● ABOVE This was taken in a studio. Care was needed to keep the light from casting the mother's shadow onto the child. Placing the child behind the mother has created an informal mood and it looks as if a game is in progress. Try to make pictures look fun, especially in the artificial conditions of the studio.

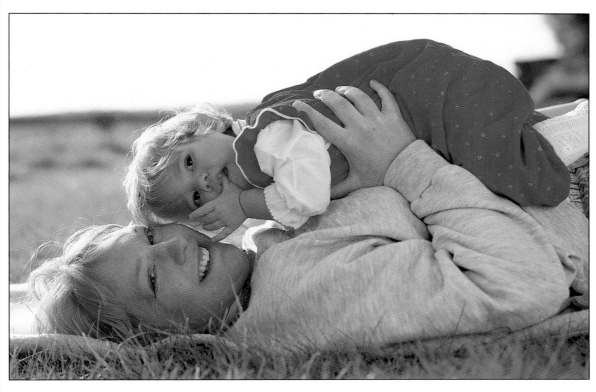

● LEFT This picture was taken against the light and a reflector was used to bounce light back onto the mother and child. This has given a soft halo effect to their hair and made the picture look warm and summery. Asking them to lie down on the grass has further increased the air of a natural bond between mother and child. The low viewpoint makes the viewer feel part of the picture.

● RIGHT Draping a white sheet over the window has created a very soft background. The mother and child were lit by flash softened by a diffuser. This has softened the overall effect even more, perfectly fitting the mood. In this case the baby was fascinated by the flash light, and it proved a useful diversion for him. Using a 100 mm lens allowed a comfortable distance between the camera and the subject.

● LEFT Going in very close has achieved an intimate picture of a mother and her son. It was taken on a chilly autumn day, and they are huddled together to give a snug effect. In such situations take care that the child does not get too cold and become distressed.

BABIES AND YOUNG CHILDREN

Photographs of young children can bring pleasure to many people, not only their parents and close relatives.

The important thing to remember is that young children tire easily. Patience will be needed to get the best out of what might be a very brief photographic session. If the child seems to be becoming unhappy it is best to take a break and restart at a later time. Try to avoid dressing young children up in strange costumes, as these can humiliate them. The child should be having fun, and not be made fun of.

Natural light is probably the best, as it will not distract or distress the child. Very young babies are often upset by flashlight.

Try to think ahead about backgrounds. An ugly intrusion can ruin what would otherwise be a great shot, and there may not be a chance to move the subject. As well as more formal portraits, try to photograph the young child engaged in some activity — playing, or perhaps at bathtime.

When photographing small children in a studio or away from home, have a few toys around for them to play with. They may well not be able to understand a request to go to a particular place or do something specific. Often the only way of getting the right expression from a child is to play the fool.

With children who are two years old or more, Polaroid pictures can be a great help at the photography session. They will be fascinated by seeing the results instantly, and the pictures are also useful for checking exposure, lighting and general composition.

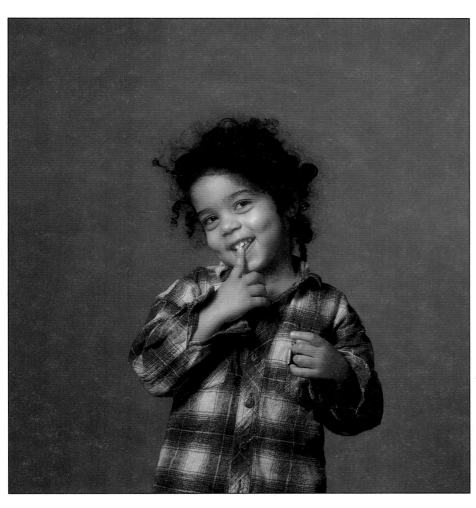

● BELOW Bathing can be fun for young children and provide plenty of opportunity for natural-looking pictures. This one was taken by standing directly over the bath and using the light coming in through a window. A standard focal length lens was used. By working quickly several good shots were taken with the minimum of fuss.

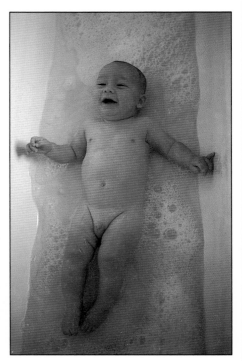

● ABOVE This child acted spontaneously for the camera in a studio which other children would have found daunting. Several shots were taken, each one with a different expression. They were lit by a flash unit which had a fast recycling time so that shots could be taken in close succession. Editing the pictures was difficult as each one had its own character, but this one was finally declared the winner.

● RIGHT Going in close on this baby's face has given full emphasis to his expression. Soft lighting has given a feeling of gentleness. A good deal of gesticulation, face pulling and cooing by the photographer and the child's parents were needed to maintain his interest. Never prolong a session with a young child to the point where it becomes upset. At the first sign of unhappiness, it is best to stop and try again later.

● LEFT The blanket makes an unusual and interesting background. Always look out for something new, so that shots taken over a period have variety. This picture was taken by natural light coming through a large window, with a reflector used to throw light back and give a fairly even level of illumination.

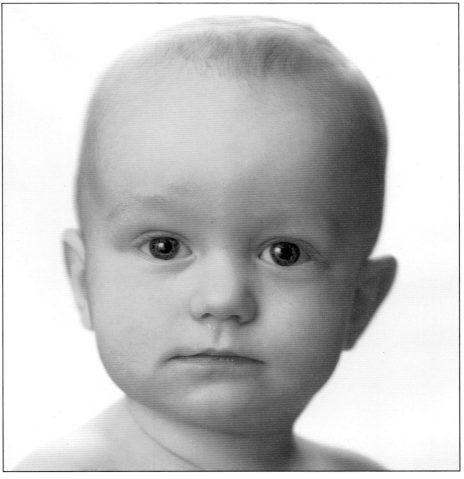

PETS

Pets are always a favourite subject. Before you start to photograph them, it is most important to realize that although pets cannot speak they do have ways of communicating. If you endlessly try to get a dog to do something it does not want to do, it is never going to look happy and the shot will betray its mood. Eventually it will snap at you or even bite. You do have to take this seriously, especially if you are using pets and children together. Both get bored quickly, and when the session is no longer a game for them, stop.

So you will need to work quickly. An autofocus lens and TTL exposure control will be an asset. Very often it is the fleeting expression that makes the shot. Going in close helps to capture this. A medium telephoto lens, say 100 mm, would be a good choice. This will help to fill the frame without getting too close to your subjects and disturbing them.

Try to avoid dressing animals up. The best shots are natural ones, not dogs wearing dresses or cats in sunglasses.

As well as shots for the album or framing, pictures of pets are ideal for Christmas and birthday cards.

Most animals grow faster than we do. Keep photographing them: taking a shot every month of your puppy or kitten will form an interesting record of its development.

● ABOVE LEFT Children with pets make very good subjects for photographs. But in both cases their attention soon wanders. When you see either tiring or becoming agitated it is time to stop.

● ABOVE RIGHT Some pets are more docile than others. This donkey in Ireland allowed plenty of time to move around and choose the best viewpoint. The background is blurred by using a wide aperture and fast shutter speed. The donkey's face is sharp and crisp, and the shot was taken just as it pricked up its ears.

● RIGHT The dog looks alert and the fishing net makes an interesting prop. Autofocus and TTL exposure metering help you to work quickly when photographing pets.

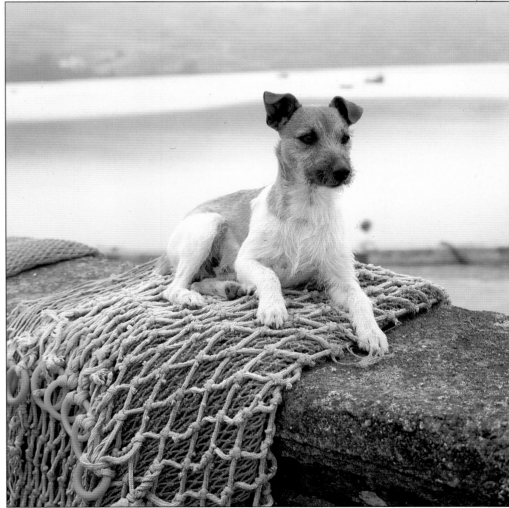

● LEFT, ABOVE AND BELOW These are ideal shots for a Christmas card. A simple prop such as the holly used here is all that was needed to set the scene. The backdrop is a graduated one shading from white to black, and the scene is lit by flash.

Pictures of people do not all have to be head and shoulders or full length. There are many other areas of the body that lend themselves to being photographed. Some of these pictures can be evocative and sensual. Others can be character studies, such as shots of gnarled hands and wrinkled skin.

Most standard lenses will not focus close enough, and a close-up attachment of some kind will be needed: extension rings, bellows or a macro lens. Close-up lenses that fit onto the front of an existing lens like a filter are available, but the quality of the image is not very good. Some telephoto lenses can also be focused to quite short distances and will give excellent close-up shots. With all these devices depth of field is very limited.

For close-up work the camera has to be kept perfectly still and it is advisable to use a tripod. In particular, extension tubes and bellows reduce the amount of light passing through the lens, so that exposures have to be long. They are made even longer by the need to use a small aperture to make the most of the available depth of field. When using available light, and with the lens stopped down to f22 or even f32, an exposure of 1 second or more may be needed. The subject also has to be kept still, which can be difficult.

If lighting a close-up picture with flash, be careful of shadows. What looks acceptable from a distance may be harsh and ugly in close-up and dominate the picture. As the camera will be only a short way from the subject, it is vital to ensure that it does not cast its own shadow onto the area.

Once the photographs have been developed, consider making enlarged prints. These could become many times larger than life size, with a strikingly abstract, sculptural quality.

● RIGHT This picture was taken with a macro lens. The subject's feet were surrounded with a white sheet so that they became isolated and dominated the picture. They were lit with flash, using a 'softbox' to diffuse the light. The angle of view gives a sculptural effect.

● LEFT Going in close on this girl's hand, with her own body as the background, has created a sensual picture. A 100 mm lens focused at its nearest distance was used – this shows that close-ups are possible without special lenses or accessories.

● LEFT This picture was taken using a combination of extension rings and macro lens. The girl's eye was approximately 5 cm (2 in) from the front of the lens. It was essential to mount the lens on a tripod and to have a support for the girl's head. The picture was lit by flash and the depth of field, even at f22, was virtually non-existent.